More

THE USER'
SPIRITUAL TEACHERS

"An important resource for both beginners and more seasoned practitioners—presented with wisdom, clarity, and lightness."
—ZUIKO REDDING, Cedar Rapids Zen Center

"A wonderful resource. This guide is down-to-earth and offers a broader perspective about what to expect and what not to expect from spiritual teachers."
—DAVID RYNICK, author of *This Truth Never Fails*

"Finally, a well thought-out, easy-to-read guide to help folks assess whether a given teacher may be prone to abuse his power over them or is genuinely interested in empowering them."
—TIM BURKETT, author of *Nothing Holy about It*

"Scott Edelstein helps us to stay wide-awake to the obstacles on the thorny path of spiritual companionship with another human being."
—MELISSA MYOZEN BLACKER, coeditor of *The Book of Mu*

THE **USER'S GUIDE** TO
spiritual teachers

SCOTT EDELSTEIN

OPEN YOUR HEART. DISCERN THE TRUTH. PRACTICE WISELY.

Wisdom

Wisdom Publications
199 Elm Street
Somerville, MA 02144 USA
wisdompubs.org

Library of Congress Cataloging-in-Publication Data
Names: Edelstein, Scott, author.
Title: The user's guide to spiritual teachers / by Scott Edelstein.
Description: Somerville, MA : Wisdom Publications, 2017.
Identifiers: LCCN 2016028183 (print) | LCCN 2016038731 (ebook)
  | ISBN 9780861716104 (pbk. : alk. paper) | ISBN 0861716108
  (pbk. : alk. paper) | ISBN 9781614294184 () | ISBN 1614294186 ()
Subjects: LCSH: Spiritual life—Study and teaching. | Religious educators.
Classification: LCC BL42 .E34 2017 (print) | LCC
  BL42 (ebook) | DDC 206/.1—dc23
LC record available at https://lccn.loc.gov/2016028183

ISBN 978-0-86171-610-4   ebook ISBN 978-1-61429-418-4

21 20 19 18 17
5 4 3 2 1

Cover design by Phil Pascuzzo. Interior design by Kristin
Goble. Set in Adobe Garamond Pro 10.5/14.

Wisdom Publications' books are printed on acid-free paper and meet
the guidelines for permanence and durability of the Production
Guidelines for Book Longevity of the Council on Library Resources.

🌺 This book was produced with environmental mindfulness.
For more information, please visit wisdompubs.org/wisdom-environment.

Printed in the United States of America.

Please visit fscus.org.

Table of Contents

My heart skipped a beat and then flat-out tripped over itself and fell on its face. Then my heart stood up, brushed itself off, took a deep breath and announced: "I want a spiritual teacher." . . . *My God, but I wanted a spiritual teacher.*

ELIZABETH GILBERT, FROM HER MEMOIR
EAT, PRAY, LOVE

An enlightened person is someone who embodies the deep understanding of nonduality while acting in accordance with ordinary boundaries, not being bound to either realm but acting freely and harmoniously.

ZEN MASTER DOGEN

The truth will set you free, but first it will piss you off.

JOE KLAAS (POPULARIZED BY GLORIA STEINEM)

There's a seeker born every minute.

"HAPPY" HARRY COX,
FROM THE FIRESIGN THEATRE'S
EVERYTHING YOU KNOW IS WRONG

How This Book Can Help

Welcome.

If you're like most readers of this book, you picked it up because you're feeling two strong pulls.

The first pull is a stirring inside you—an internal pressure to live a deeper life, to become more of the person you were meant to be. Maybe it's an urge to deepen your connection with others, with yourself, with the world, or with God (in whatever way you define God). Or perhaps it's some urgent, recurring question about your mission or place in life. Or maybe it's a call to look closely and honestly at some of the most basic dilemmas of being human.

You can feel this force inside you, pushing you toward something larger than yourself, toward completeness—even though you may not know in what direction to move or what spiritual path to follow.

The second pull is the need for one-to-one spiritual direction.

You might already meditate, pray, chant, or engage in some other spiritual practice. You might read philosophy, or spiritual essays, or the writings of people such as Rumi or Thich Nhat Hanh or Thérèse of Lisieux or Rabbi Nachman of Breslau. But you also yearn for more: spiritual guidance from a perceptive, caring, trustworthy human being.

Ideally, this person can point out the spiritual choices that present themselves to you and the likely consequences of selecting each one. They can help you see the trajectory you're traveling and the opportunities and difficulties that may lie ahead. They can help you navigate the often-stormy waters of your own heart and mind. They can help you regain your spiritual footing when you slip and tumble. They can address your most pressing spiritual questions, concerns, and fears. And they can help you discover—and take up—your unique place and purpose in the world.

You might feel strongly that you'll find this person within the religious tradition in which you were raised. Or you might feel just the opposite: that you need to explore one or more traditions that have been unfamiliar to you. Or you might feel caught somewhere in between, not sure where to look or just what to look for.

Regardless of your background, however, you feel—like so many of us—that you cannot move forward entirely on your own. You need the help of someone who has walked the path before you, who can help point the way.

Such a person is usually called a spiritual teacher—or, sometimes, a spiritual counselor, coach, director, or mentor. (In this book, for clarity's sake, I'll call all these people spiritual teachers.)

In the wired, webbed life of the twenty-first century, all of us have a huge array of these teachers to choose from. Not surprisingly, they range from enormously helpful to actively harmful. Yet we can't go shopping for a spiritual teacher the way we would for a florist or a caterer or a shoe repair shop, because the opening of the human heart can't be treated like a service or a commodity.

It's important to feel an affinity with your spiritual teacher. This rarely comes just from reading someone's books, watching their videos, or exploring their website. You'll need to carefully discern whether someone is a good spiritual teacher for *you*. (You of course get to make mistakes, change teachers, or both.) Often this process involves slow discovery, trial and error, and lots of uncertainty.

This uncertainty may include a whole raft of questions. For example, what qualifications should you look for in a spiritual teacher? What attributes of a teacher genuinely matter, and which ones don't matter much? How can you tell a good spiritual teacher from a less helpful one—or from someone who's a fraud, a predator, or mentally ill? Can the same spiritual teacher be great for one person but terrible for another? What's the etiquette for asking someone to be your spiritual teacher? Can your regular minister, priest, or rabbi become your spiritual teacher? Are these even the right questions to ask?

And once you've become someone's student, what will you be expected to do or commit to? Should you feel a binding sense of loyalty to the teacher, or are you free to go elsewhere at any time? Can you have two or more different teachers at once? If so, how do you navigate the relationships?

After you've found a good teacher, how do you build a strong, healthy, and mutually respectful relationship with them? What can you do to make the most of that relationship? And what can you do to avoid the dangers and dilemmas that often arise, such as idealizing the teacher, imagining that they know more than they do, or expecting them to solve your biggest problems for you?

Beyond that, what are the warning signs that something about your relationship with a teacher isn't right? At what point does someone stop being a teacher and start becoming a cult leader? When does being someone's student stunt rather than encourage your growth?

Then there are the nuts-and-bolts questions. Is it okay for a spiritual teacher to charge money? To ask you questions about your personal life? To treat one student differently from another? How do you balance the requirements of spiritual practice or study with the needs of your family and the demands of your work?

And what about your most profound spiritual questions—the ones that put you on this path in the first place? Is there a right and a wrong way to bring them to a spiritual teacher? Should you expect direct answers, or guidance in finding those answers yourself, or simply a refocusing or reframing of those questions?

Perhaps most important, what can you do to support your efforts—and the efforts of your teacher—so that you become fully yourself and a deeply positive force in the world?

If these are the kind of questions you're asking—welcome. You're in the right place and reading the right book.

This book won't answer your deepest religious and spiritual questions for you. But it *will* answer most of the questions I've listed above—and it will give you the tools, information, and guidance you need to answer many more for yourself.

The words *spiritual* and *spirituality* mean many different things to different people. One person thinks spirituality means getting a rush up their spine. Another thinks it means communicating with angels. A third thinks it's about sitting cross-legged until their legs go numb. A fourth thinks it's about volunteering at a soup kitchen.

In this book I use the word *spirituality* sparingly, preferring other, more specific words whenever possible. I use the adjective *spiritual* more often—almost always in the context of spiritual teachers, leaders, traditions, organizations, and so on. In my use of these words, they refer to any activity that is meant to make us more aware, more human, and more whole.

Whenever you hear anyone use the words *spiritual* and *spirituality*, know that the words have a profusion of meanings. It's worth asking the speaker how they define those terms.

It would be unreasonable of me to expect you to take everything I say on faith—and just as unwise for you to follow my guidance without first knowing who I am.

For the past forty years I've studied spirituality and religion—and Buddhism and Judaism in particular—with several spiritual teachers. In all cases, the relationships have been positive and productive—though, like everyone, I've had my share of challenges and spiritual crises.

I've also been fortunate to have several friends who are spiritual teachers. I've spent a great deal of time with these people outside of their formal roles as teachers—in their homes, on social occasions, and in many restaurants and bars. In addition, I've been privileged to serve as editor and literary agent for four spiritual teachers.

I'm a committed proponent of serious spirituality in all forms and traditions. I've also been a member of Methodist, Quaker, Zen, and Jewish congregations. I'm the author of over a dozen books that help people to deepen and open their lives. My writing on spiritual topics has also been published in a variety of magazines, books, and other media.

One thing I'm not, however, is a spiritual teacher. I'm simply someone who has been in several long-term student-teacher relationships; who has closely observed many other such relationships; who has interacted with many spiritual teachers off duty; and who is able to write about student-teacher relationships honestly and, I hope, articulately.

Please read my words with an open mind—and take them with a pinch of salt. Accept what feels wholesome, right, and useful—and set aside what doesn't. When, on occasion, I become emphatic, it's to stress the seriousness of what I have to say, not to demand your obedience. When I repeatedly emphasize a few key themes, my intent is to underscore their importance and subtlety, not to express doubt about your ability to pay attention.

Here is my most vital advice for learning from any spiritual teacher. Show up; pay close attention to what you see and hear; then test it all against what your heart, mind, and gut tell you. This mindful discernment is the single most important skill for navigating any student-teacher relationship—as well as the turbulent waters of life in general.

Ultimately, you will discover that you are the one who must do the work; the teacher can only point the way and remind you of what you already know.

Journey wisely. Journey well.

Basic Wisdom

Don't go by reports, by legends, by traditions, by scripture, by logical conjecture, by inference, by analogies, by agreement through pondering views, by probability, or by the thought, "This contemplative is our teacher." When you know for yourselves that "These qualities are skillful; these qualities are blameless; these qualities are praised by the wise; these qualities, when adopted and carried out, lead to welfare and to happiness"—then you should enter and remain in them.

BUDDHA

Life is not a problem to be solved. It is a blessing to be celebrated.

JOAN CHITTISTER

A true spiritual teacher does not have anything to teach in the conventional sense of the word, does not have anything to give or add to you, such as new information, beliefs, or rules of conduct. The only function of such a teacher is to help you remove that which separates you from the truth.... The words are no more than signposts.

ECKHART TOLLE

There are a thousand ways to kneel and kiss the ground; there are a thousand ways to go home again.

RUMI

A spiritual teacher is a living, breathing human being, with normal human emotions, impulses, and desires.

It's easy to imagine that spiritual teachers are different from us in some basic way—that they have somehow transcended fear, loneliness, grief, and all the other emotions most of us work so hard to suppress or avoid.

In my own early days with spiritual teachers, I imagined that they were happy and serene more or less all the time. I couldn't accept what should have been obvious: that they feel the same emotional pain (and pleasure) that all of us do. I also couldn't see that, *unlike* so many of us, the best of them don't expend much effort trying to avoid the pain or grab on to the pleasure. Instead, they let their emotions—pleasant and unpleasant—arise, pass through them, and blow away like fog.

This is what many of the best spiritual teachers will help *you* learn to do as well.

An authentic spiritual teacher is concerned with both helping you and serving the world.
Spiritual and religious practices are much more than self-improvement—though self-improvement is often one of their fruits.

When I first began studying with a spiritual teacher, I wanted to acquire all kinds of goodies: insight, wisdom, inner peace, mental clarity, and heightened spiritual health. I even wanted to get really good at transcending myself.

Every one of these goals was about *me* and the spiritual booty I hoped to accumulate. Part of the job of my first two teachers was to help me see the acquisitiveness of the approach I was taking. Another part was to help me realize my inseparability from the rest of the world—and to see that, as human beings, we must serve as well as be served.

Today, many spiritual teachers promote spirituality as a way to relax, reduce stress, or create more personal power or effectiveness. While there's nothing wrong with learning these—or any other useful skill—they do little to help us see beyond our habitual, narrow definitions of ourselves and our roles in the world.

Some spiritual teachers can do much more: they can help us grow more deeply into ourselves and be of greater service to the world. And as we serve the world, doing what we are called to do—whether it's designing a helpful newsletter, teaching kids basic financial skills, or being with people as they die—we can forget ourselves and, paradoxically, become ourselves more completely.

Perhaps the ancient sage Hillel said it best: "If I am not for myself, who will be for me? And if I am only for myself, what am I?"

Learning from spiritual teachers means building a personal relationship with them—but this doesn't always mean you have to live (or travel to) where they are.

In a person-to-person relationship with a spiritual teacher, you'll typically pose questions, ask for spiritual guidance, and learn from the teacher's actions, words, and way of being. The teacher, in turn, will get to know your needs, habits, inclinations, and ways of thinking and being. This will enable them to be as helpful to you as possible.

Although this process usually involves some regular face-to-face contact, some teachers and students who are separated by long distances communicate quite effectively by Skype, FaceTime, phone, letters, or email. So don't let distance or national borders discourage you. If you'd like to study with someone long distance, ask if that might be possible.

That said, a student-teacher relationship rarely grows in a vacuum. The great majority of spiritual teachers are part of spiritual communities. Being actively engaged in such a community, even long distance, has many additional benefits and challenges. (I'll discuss these in some detail in chapter 8.) Ask your teacher how this engagement might be possible, in spite of your physical distance.

Also never forget that, with or without the support of a spiritual community, the world in front of your face can teach you a great deal. You don't have to trek halfway around the world to find wisdom.

Be careful not to judge spiritual teachers by their day jobs.

The great majority of spiritual teachers work at something in addition to their teaching or mentoring. Some lead congregations. Others work at jobs where they connect to other human hearts, minds, and/or bodies as therapists, bodyworkers, healers, or secular teachers.

However, some very good teachers have entirely unrelated day jobs. I've known spiritual teachers whose day jobs included van driver, soybean researcher, special effects designer, housewife, and animal control officer. Usually teachers hold these jobs for the same reasons most of us do: to pay the bills and to keep themselves and their families fed.

It's best not to worry about what a spiritual teacher does to earn a living (provided it's honest and honorable). Do, however, carefully observe how they live their life. While it's unfair (and foolish) to expect them to be perfect, they *should* be sane, ethical, and compassionate. The more integrated and wholesome their life is, and the more they seem to live by what they teach, the more valuable their teaching is likely to be.

That said, many good spiritual teachers spend long hours in their teaching roles—and, as a result, they don't always get the sleep, relaxation, or leisure they need. Some may urge people to take good care of their own health; then they go home, sleep only a few hours, and get up and go straight back to work. Many otherwise wise and grounded spiritual teachers struggle with this occupational hazard.

Don't judge a spiritual teacher by how well known they are, how many books they have published, or how many students they have.
Like members of all professions, spiritual teachers range from wise, authentic, and wonderfully helpful to incompetent, deeply deluded, or outright fraudulent. They also, of course, range from internationally famous to unknown.

Although fame and ability often go together, sometimes the opposite is the case. In fact, charismatic charlatans, predators, and narcissists often attract very large numbers of followers.

When making a decision about a spiritual teacher, it's best to ignore their popularity (or lack of it). Instead, observe them carefully as you and others interact with them, and evaluate what you see with your own heart and mind.

It's also a good idea to ask about a teacher's experience, training, and formal credentials. For example, who was (or is) their own teacher? Where, for how long, and with whom did they study or train? Have they been formally authorized to teach? If so, by what person or institution? Do they have a degree, certificate, or other such credential? How long have they been teaching?

Of course, credentials and experience don't tell the whole story. Most of us know some incompetent, uncompassionate people who have first-class formal credentials—as well as some very wise and talented folks with few such credentials. So by all means dig for information, but trust the messages from your head, heart, and gut most of all.

In general, good spiritual teachers have considerable talents and insight in addition to (or, in rare cases, instead of) official credentials and experience. If a teacher lacks such credentials or experience, it's a good idea to be extremely cautious. But it's also wise to look beyond those credentials, to qualities and abilities that matter even more: humility, wisdom, compassion, transparency, openness, and a willingness to serve.

Every spiritual teacher makes mistakes, both large and small.

All human beings are fallible, precisely because they're human. Being ordained as a priest or monk or nun—or having formal credentials as a spiritual teacher—doesn't change this.

Even the wisest and most experienced spiritual teachers make the same kind—and often the same amount—of everyday errors as the rest of us. So don't be surprised or shocked when they overcook the oatmeal, drop a vase, give you poor directions, say "uncle" when they mean "cousin," or back their car into a telephone pole.

Your teacher may also make some small but well-intentioned mistakes in guiding you—for example, recommending a book that you find unhelpful and dull, or emphasizing a certain point because they've confused you with someone else. If they do this occasionally, forgive them (and correct them as necessary). If they do it repeatedly, however, or if their mistake is a significant one—such as prescribing a spiritual practice that ultimately injures you—speak to them directly about it. If necessary, consider finding a different teacher.

How a teacher handles their mistakes will also teach you a great deal about them. If they recognize and admit to their mistakes quickly, that's a positive sign. If they also speak publicly about their weaknesses, limitations, and blind spots, that's even better.

In contrast, a teacher who rarely says "I was wrong" or "I'm sorry" or "I don't know" will often get themselves and their students into deep, painful trouble.

Every teacher has some bad habits, physical flaws, eccentric interests, and harmless quirks. Subconsciously, many of us believe that a good spiritual teacher doesn't do any of the minor things we might personally disapprove of—e.g., drink alcohol, smoke, overeat, or support a different political party than we do. In real life, though, they often do. When it comes to such minor things, set aside your disapproval as best you can.

But when it comes to genuinely important issues—such as living by what they teach or treating their students with respect—let your discernment guide you.

We may also imagine that spiritual insight somehow generates physical attractiveness, good luck, youthfulness, excellent physical health, or protection from physical harm. And we might assume that every worthy spiritual teacher has a good deal of charisma, and/or first-rate speaking and presenting skills.

Yet spiritual insight is not particularly related to any of the above. Many good teachers do have lots of charisma, but others are humble and unassuming. Some are very good speakers and presenters—but, in many cases, they built those skills long before becoming spiritual teachers.

Certainly it's a good idea to avoid—or run away from—any teacher who is a practicing addict, or who seems self-centered or mentally unbalanced. Otherwise, though, let your teacher be eccentric. Give yourself the same permission as well.

There's nothing wrong with a spiritual teacher charging money for what they do, so long as their fees are reasonable and transparent.
A spiritual teacher's time and effort are valuable, just as yours are. Why shouldn't they be entitled to charge reasonable fees and to make an honest (but not lavish) living from them?

That said, a spiritual teacher's mission is to help people live deeper lives and serve the world. If you sense that a teacher is simply trying to maximize their revenue, think seriously about finding a new teacher.

Some spiritual teachers don't charge set fees at all. Instead, they put out a donation box, along with a small sign that says something like, "Teachings are given freely; financial contributions are accepted gratefully." This is an elegant and simple way to accommodate all serious students, regardless of their financial circumstances.

In any case, a spiritual teacher should be honest and transparent about where their money comes from. When someone is paid a salary by their organization, community, or tradition—which is the case for many teachers—the amount of that salary should be public information. If it isn't, take this as an enormous red flag.

A good teacher will help you become more of who you are, not less.
A good teacher won't try to order you around, tell you what to think, make you into a robot, or treat you like a child. They also won't offer you Brownie points for pleasing them or jumping through spiritual hoops. When the two of you are together, they will be fully present, both intellectually and emotionally. And they will hear and respond to your questions, not merely pose their own.

Spiritual study and practices aren't meant to turn you into a clone of your teacher. Instead, they should deepen your connection to the world and to a power greater than yourself. Ultimately, this will make you more yourself, not more like your teacher.

Of course, if you're on a retreat or living in a monastic setting, you'll be expected to follow a set of rules and limitations regarding what you do and say. So long as these do no harm, and are applied more or less equally to everyone, then please do follow them while you're in residence.

But if a teacher routinely orders you around—or picks out your spouse or career for you, or otherwise tries to micromanage you or take control of any significant aspect of your personal life—back away. There's a good chance you're dealing with someone dangerous.

Many of us students try to avoid the unavoidable pain of making our own decisions, living into their consequences, and growing up. So we ask our teachers to make our personal decisions for us: *Should I take this job or that job? Should I leave my husband or stay with him and try to work things out? Is it okay for me to eat meat? Should I go to the week-long retreat or not?*

But answering such questions isn't their job. In fact, a good teacher will refuse to make a decision for you that you need to make on your own—and will hand the power and responsibility back to you. They may also help you examine your own emotions and uncertainty around the issue.

We each need to make the best real-life choices we can, pay close attention to what happens, and then make further choices. Indeed, this is the very essence of spiritual practice.

Some years ago I felt very much at a spiritual crossroads. I was living several hundred miles away from my ex-teacher, with whom I had not spoken for nearly three years. On a visit to his hometown, however, I stopped in to see him.

After catching up on our lives for a bit, I explained that I was confused and that I felt pulled in two directions. I didn't know whether to stay where I was living or return and become his student once again.

The answer I expected was, "Come back here and learn from me some more. It will be good for you." But a part of me also expected the opposite: "Stay where you are. You've put down roots there."

I was wrong on both counts. With a serious expression on his face, the teacher said, "Come back when you feel you have no other choice."

In that one brief sentence, he handed the decision back to me, where it belonged. For who else would truly know when I had no other choice?

An authentic teacher will expect you to test and mull over what they teach you, not merely accept it on faith.

Don't mindlessly believe anything. Test it out against your own experience. Then, if it holds up—if it resonates with your experience and observation—have faith in it. If it doesn't, question it—or question the teacher.

You will discover that, over time, this testing and questioning will serve you well—not just in your relationship with your teacher, but in almost every relationship and situation. Eventually this process will become second nature, and you will have developed faith in your own powers of observation and discernment.

No legitimate spiritual tradition says, "Believe and do everything you're told—and never think about it, discuss it, test it, or challenge it." This is the case even among religious traditions that place a strong emphasis on faith and obedience. The most fundamentalist Christian in America doesn't say, "Turn the other cheek! Don't try to understand what Jesus meant by it—just do it!"

In most cases, in fact, the opposite is true: we must regularly examine our own faith and spiritual life—and periodically revise them—in order for them to remain vital.

It's important to question the beliefs we were raised with—but it's equally important not to stop there. The process of questioning needs to go on continuously. Otherwise we end up living our lives according to a new batch of untested beliefs.

Faith plays an essential role in any religious inquiry. But the strongest and most nourishing faith results from considering, examining, and testing a spiritual teaching or practice over time—and, through your own experience, discovering it to be valuable, true, and trustworthy.

A good teacher has no trouble saying, "I don't know." They may even emphasize the importance of uncertainty and not knowing.
When we're ignorant, and know in our hearts that we're ignorant, that's when we're best able to learn. It's when we think we know something that we can most stand in our own way. And it's when we're 100 percent convinced that we're right that we may do the most harm—to others and to ourselves.

Many spiritual teachers and traditions remind us that not knowing is a part of the human condition. Some even stress that not knowing can be profoundly valuable. Jewish mystics write of the *ein sof,* which cannot be known or described. A Christian spiritual classic, *The Cloud of Unknowing*, mentions "a cloud of unknowing betwixt thee and God" and urges us to "smite upon that thick cloud of unknowing with a sharp dart of love." Zen teacher Shunryu Suzuki wrote of the importance of living with an open, unknowing "beginner's mind," rather than with the knowledge-filled mind of an expert.

There are things that we human beings simply cannot know. We can never know precisely when we will die, or exactly what will happen a year, a day, an hour, or a minute from now. This uncertainty is built into the very fabric of our lives. A good teacher will acknowledge this—and perhaps even emphasize it.

Not knowing isn't shameful. It may even be a state of grace.

An authentic spiritual teacher respects personal boundaries—and will expect you to do the same. Many teachers and traditions tell us that our sense of separateness from others is an illusion. Still, illusion or not, we can't all share one car or apartment or bank account. The world of things and boundaries never goes away, even if we see its illusory nature.

In practice, this means that your teacher shouldn't touch you in ways or places that you don't want to be touched, or know things about you that you don't want them to know. And they don't get to tell you things about themselves that you don't clearly agree to hear. (They do get to ask for your permission when they sense that they may be approaching a boundary or a sensitive topic—e.g., "Are you okay if I ask you some questions about your childhood?" Remember, though, you get to say no. In fact, if something about the request doesn't feel right, it may be *wise* to say no.)

Personal boundary issues do sometimes arise between well-intentioned spiritual teachers and their students. One example: some spiritual teachers occasionally hug their students, or hold their hands, or even kiss them on the cheek or forehead. Many people find this loving or charming. But if you don't want your teacher doing it with you, ask them not to. Be clear and direct about this. If they ignore your requests, or repeatedly forget them, or dismiss your concerns, you've learned something important: that your teacher is at best careless or disrespectful, and at worst uncaring or exploitive.

Respecting personal boundaries is a two-way street, of course. You may feel moved to hug your teacher, or tell them some of your secrets, or give them an expensive gift of appreciation. But if they ask you not to, take that request seriously and honor it graciously.

The issue of sexual boundaries is far less ambiguous. If your teacher asks or pressures you to have sex with them, the wisest thing to do is to say no, firmly and explicitly. I also recommend finding another teacher. And if their response is something like, "You have an intimacy problem; I'm helping you break through it," or "Don't worry—we used to be husband and wife in a previous life," or "It's okay, it's all part of the training," get away fast. You're in the presence of a predator. It may also be a good idea to report their actions to their superior.

Be equally wary of a teacher who tells you (perhaps repeatedly) that you're their favorite, or that you have unique abilities or insight or potential, or that you are special in some other way. In student-teacher relationships, this is a common prelude to a seduction. An authentic teacher might praise you on occasion, but they won't repeatedly flatter you.

No spiritual teacher, even a highly talented one, is going to solve your problems for you. When we first begin learning from a spiritual teacher, we may assume they will staunch our pain or solve our problems. But neither of these is part of their job.

A spiritual teacher can help you see more clearly, point out where you're stuck, offer a perspective that will help you make your own decision, or—sometimes—suggest a specific course of action. But you're the one who has to live your life.

Here's some very good news, courtesy of several of my teachers: once you let go of the idea that your teacher can (or should) solve your problems for you, your view of life—and your engagement with it—will become wider and deeper.

Much of what some spiritual teachers say may seem confusing at first.

Some aspects of human life—and the world—can't be expressed in easy sound bites. For this reason, many of our greatest spiritual teachers have relied on poetry, songs, parables, fables, metaphors, koans, and other indirect forms of language.

Sometimes a spiritual lesson can be bewildering even when it's in simple, straightforward sentences. Consider these words of Jesus: "I tell you not to resist an evil person. But whoever slaps you on your right cheek, turn the other to him also." Christians continue to wrestle with these words after twenty centuries.

Or consider this statement from an ancient Chinese Zen teacher:

> Before I had studied meditation for thirty years, I saw mountains as mountains, and waters as waters. When I arrived at a more intimate knowledge, I came to the point where I saw that mountains are not mountains, and waters are not waters. But now that I have got its very substance, I am at rest. For it's just that I see mountains once again as mountains, and waters once again as waters.

One of my own teachers used to say: "Two plus two is four. But sometimes it's eight. Sometimes ninety. Sometimes the color green."

In part, he was being metaphorical. But he was also being literal. If you release two pairs of field mice, two males and two females, onto an island with few predators and plenty of food, in a few months the island will have hundreds of mice, not four pairs. Or take an electron: common sense tells us that if you shoot it toward two slits in a piece of paper spaced six inches apart, it can only go through one of them. But in fact, as multiple physics experiments have demonstrated, it somehow goes through both at once.

Most of us students compulsively seek explanations. But reality doesn't need an explanation. It's already here. We would be wiser to focus on how things are than clamor for explanations for them.

When a spiritual teacher says something odd or counterintuitive or downright weird, don't write it off or ignore it. Don't just try to figure it out logically, either. Ask the teacher to say more about it. Question them about it. Meditate with it; wrestle with it; chew on it; let it soak into you. One day it may burst open like a flower.

If your teacher is from a different country or culture, you may have trouble separating their spiritual tradition from their culture.

Over the centuries, all of the world's major religions have adapted to a wide range of cultures. But whenever a tradition moves into a new culture, there is a transition period during which some of the old cultural trappings are abandoned, some are adapted, some are replaced, and some are maintained without change.

This process of adaptation is now occurring all around the world with every major religion. While this spiritual cross-pollination will ultimately be very helpful, in the short run it creates confusion, particularly when living teachers take their traditions to other countries and cultures.

For example, if you attend a talk by the Dalai Lama, you'll see him dressed in an orange robe, sitting cross-legged on a stage full of bright colors. He might talk about the Four Noble Truths, the Eightfold Path, and a person named the Karmapa. You'll probably have no idea how much of this is classical Buddhism, how much is Tibetan Buddhism, and how much is adapted from the indigenous Tibetan religion of Bön. (For the record, the bright colors come from Bön but are now also parts of Tibetan Buddhism. The robe and the cross-legged posture developed in classical India but have slight Tibetan variations. The Karmapa is unique to Tibetan Buddhism. The Four Noble Truths and the Eightfold Path are common throughout all schools of Buddhism.)

All of this can be very difficult to sort out. Your best course is to observe carefully, but not jump to any conclusions about what is essential to the tradition and what is a cultural variation or addition. Over time, and with experience, you'll begin to separate the religious teachings and traditions from the cultural ones—or at least you will understand more clearly how the two intertwine. You will also no longer mistake the exotic for the spiritual, or imagine that adopting the customs of another culture will have a magical and profound effect on your life.

A teacher who is ideal for you may not be right for your partner, your best friend, or your kid.
Each of us has our own interests, obsessions, fears, and burning spiritual questions. Some of us do better when we're gently coaxed, others when we're vigorously challenged. Some of us want a teacher who speaks primarily to our heart; others lean toward teachers who first engage our intellect. Some of us want to closely study sacred texts; others focus naturally on everyday ethics, devotion, and service. Some of us are especially drawn to mystical teachings; others want to hear about practical applications of those teachings.

It's wise, then, to select a spiritual teacher based on your own interests and inner promptings, rather than those of your partner, child, or best friend.

In the same vein, it's not a good idea to pressure someone else to study with your own teacher, no matter how wise, helpful, and fascinating you consider that teacher to be. You might be guiding someone you care about in a direction that is—for them—unhelpful. You might also end up harming or complicating your own relationship with them.

A good spiritual teacher never stops studying, practicing, and growing. Often they have a teacher of their own.
As many teachers have pointed out, spiritual study and practice offer us no finish line, no ultimate graduation ceremony. Indeed, often the distinctions between the journey and the traveler become quite blurred. Because a good teacher knows this in their bones, their own spiritual study and practice never end.

When a spiritual teacher has a teacher of their own, this isn't a sign of weakness or immaturity. Instead, it's often a sign of humility and openness— perhaps the two most important characteristics of any good spiritual teacher. It also means they are grounded in a tradition and a personal lineage.

Most spiritual teachers are less concerned with imparting information than they are with reminding you of what is already in your heart.
Your own heart, body, mind, and gut are where your spiritual study will resonate. They are where you will

discern what is of value and what is not. And they are where you and a good spiritual teacher will meet, over and over.

Expectations, Assumptions, and Misconceptions

What the mind doesn't understand, it worships or fears.

ALICE WALKER

Spiritual practice is conspiratorial rather than inspirational; it conspires to strip away everything you use to maintain the illusion of certainty, security, and self-identity.

RAMI SHAPIRO

The Thing we tell of can never be found by seeking, yet only seekers find it.

BAYAZID BISTAMI

If you think you're so enlightened, go spend a week with your family.

RAM DASS

Your teacher won't give you the Answer.
It's not that there's no Answer—but it doesn't come in a neatly wrapped description or explanation.

Even the world's best spiritual teacher can't give us a perfect recipe for enlightenment, or happiness, or living a life that matters. Nor can they explain human life to us—though we may want or ask them to. Life *can't* be explained, because it's not a concept. It's an endlessly unfolding process.

What a good teacher *can* do is help us see this process more clearly—and act in ways that support human sanity, health, and happiness.

In any case, what explanation can possibly remove the ache in your heart—or the confusion in your mind? That can only come from seeing things for yourself, not by listening to someone else's explanation.

We can't give our partners the perfect explanation that will make them love and trust us for a lifetime. But we can show them all the love and respect and wisdom we can, day by day and year by year.

We can't give our kids an explanation that will ensure that they will grow up happy, healthy, and successful. But we can honor, support, love, and teach them, while accepting that they need to make their own mistakes and learn the most important (and painful) lessons on their own.

We can come to each moment with mindfulness, openness, humility, and curiosity. If we do this consistently, over time we will begin to live into the Answer. But it won't come in the form of a simplistic explanation or a step-by-step instruction manual.

Your teacher may not give you much praise or many rewards.

It's not a spiritual teacher's job to hand out praise or other rewards for good behavior. Nor is it their job to please their students.

However, it *is* their job to help their students grow into themselves and see the world more clearly. These things can't be encouraged with gold stars or "attaboys" or "you go, girls." Each of us needs to make the effort on our own. And we need to do it for the sake of doing it, not for some other payoff.

External rewards can be powerful motivators if we're training animals or young people. The carrot-on-a-stick approach has a great track record for helping kids and four-legged creatures develop good habits.

Still, when it comes to our kids, we also want them to discover the value of practicing certain habits for their own sake. We hope that what begins as grabbing for the gold ring eventually becomes a willingness to stretch and reach out.

That's why the best spiritual teachers don't traffic in gold rings or carrots on sticks. A grownup who has begun to explore life's most important questions may want praise, recognition, a cool title, a special outfit, or some other form of spiritual candy. They may even beg for it. But an authentic teacher doesn't hand out treats in exchange for students' compliance.

Many of us come to spiritual inquiry with a desire to achieve or accomplish something. *I want to be a better Christian. I want to become my teacher's most trusted disciple. I want to transcend my ego. I want to be less caught up in desire.* We build our own carrot-and-stick devices and then expect our teachers to hold them out in front of us. But the best teachers won't touch those sticks. They will, however, help us up when we trip on them and fall on our faces. They will also offer their best encouragement and guidance—and, often, some perspective. Possibly even some humor.

Your teacher may guide you in one direction, yet guide a different student in another.
Every student and every situation is unique. So is every moment.

Guidance from a spiritual teacher should be consistently compassionate and wise. But the specifics of that guidance may change from one person—and one situation—to the next.

Diversity is a blessing. It's also built into the fabric of life. If we find it confusing or threatening, then it's our task to grow out of that confusion or fear.

Your own life path is unique—and so is everyone else's. Yet none of these paths is a solid, straight line; each one wanders and wiggles—and each wanders and wiggles differently. A good teacher can help you see where you're headed, discern the likely dangers that lie ahead, settle your body and mind, and take the next step.

Sometimes there will be other footprints on the path in front of you. At other times, you'll need to walk through unexplored territory. And, occasionally, you may see lots of footprints headed in a different direction. Your task—with your teacher's guidance—is to discern your own path and then step forward.

If your teacher uses spiritual practices, objects, or images that are unfamiliar to you, you may feel attracted to them, suspicious of them, or even both.
This is normal. Our first response to something unfamiliar can be surprise, fascination, fear, confusion, strong attraction, deep loathing, or even all six at once.

We would be wise to not take our initial response too seriously. Instead, we can investigate it and examine what's behind it. Usually we'll discover that we're holding on to some idea or expectation—often one formed long ago. Once we've identified it, we can let go of it—and begin to explore the unfamiliar with openness, curiosity, and a willingness to learn.

Be very careful about asking your spiritual teacher to fulfill more than one role in your life.
Because some spiritual teachers also work as psychotherapists, chaplains, and other helping professionals, it's possible that you'll want your teacher to work

with you in more than one capacity. This isn't inherently unethical, but it may require particular care on both people's parts.

In some cases these dual-role relationships can create problems, or at least confusion—even if both of you have the best intentions. ("Are you telling me that as my teacher or as my therapist?" "Good question. Possibly both. Actually, I'm not sure. Let me reflect on it for a couple of days.")

In some situations, the potential role conflict might be large enough that your teacher will say, "I've thought about your request and I need to say no. I won't play both roles in your life. You'll need to pick one or the other." If your teacher tells you this, it's because they have your best interests at heart. Accept their answer graciously.

You might also discern that such a multifaceted relationship isn't wise for you in practice, even if your teacher feels it's okay in principle.

Because personal and spiritual issues are often intimately intertwined, it may sometimes be difficult to discern whether to bring a particular matter to your teacher.

In such a case, go ahead and bring it up—but don't be too surprised if the teacher says, "I'm not the right person to ask about that," or "That's none of my business," or simply, "I don't know."

Often, though, those issues reflect or exemplify deeper spiritual concerns—ones involving meaning, compassion, service, uncertainty, expectations, control, letting go, relating to our fellow human beings, and finding our place in the world. A wise teacher *can*—and should—help us wrestle with these.

It's easy for us to unwittingly project our own hopes, fears, and motivations onto our teachers. This isn't pathological or neurotic; it's natural, understandable, and common. Most of us do it, more or less unconsciously, with everyone we care about. As part of our relationship with our teacher, we need to watch our own minds and actions, so that, over time, we can see for ourselves what we're doing. We need to observe our teachers carefully but not jump to conclusions about their motivations.

All of us naturally interpret what we observe. This helps us make sense of our fluid and unpredictable world. There's nothing wrong with this—*if* we're fully aware that we're doing it and hold our interpretation lightly, so that we can easily drop it when it no longer matches reality or supports our growth and sanity.

But when we cling to an interpretation even after further observation casts doubt on it, we create difficulty and confusion. And when we freeze an interpretation into a cherished belief or principle—and then demand that everyone live by it—we build a powerful engine of suffering.

A much wiser approach is to hold our interpretations and beliefs lightly, test them repeatedly, and amend or drop them in light of our further experience. It also helps to be aware of our own tendencies, limitations, hopes, fears, and desires.

Over time, some people become psychologically dependent on their teachers.
All of us who have spiritual teachers are sometimes tempted to treat them as our surrogate parents. This is especially true when we face great stress, pain, or uncertainty.

A healthy, aware spiritual teacher won't let us do this for long. They'll insist that their relationship with us be between two adults. It's the job of one adult to offer spiritual guidance to the other, and it's the other's job to carefully evaluate, consider, and test that guidance.

One easy way to spot a less-than-healthy, less-than-aware spiritual teacher is when they take on a pseudo-parent role. They make decisions for their students and encourage them to give up their own discernment and authority.

The most dangerous spiritual teachers take this to extremes, demanding childlike adoration, obedience, or dependence from their students.

In parallel fashion, a less-than-healthy student is happy—or even eager—to take on a pseudo-child role. They repeatedly refuse to shoulder the responsibility of their own discernment and authority. Instead, under the guise of "letting go," or "subverting the ego," or "accepting crazy wisdom," or the catch-all "spiritual development," they unplug their skills of observation and evaluation.

Throughout history, people have been called by the Divine to do things that defied common sense. (Even more people have been called to do things that made perfect sense—but were also challenging or frightening.) But answering a nonlogical higher calling is quite different from mindlessly following the orders of another human being—no matter what spiritual credentials they may have.

If you observe yourself seeking approval, praise, or parental advice from your spiritual teacher, recognize what you're doing and stop. If it feels appropriate, apologize. Then take these steps to recreate an adult/ adult relationship:

➤ Don't take anything your teacher says purely on faith. Look at it closely. If it doesn't look or feel or sound right, ask them about it. As appropriate, challenge it.

➤ If you're hoping to get a particular answer or outcome from your teacher (other than something such as "Yes, I can meet with you Tuesday afternoon"), ask yourself why. Do you really want their guidance, or are you actually seeking their praise or recognition or approval—or simply their attention? Don't go on a fishing expedition disguised as an inquiry. Of course, it's fine to tell your teacher what you're thinking and ask for their take on it. But be straightforward and honest about what you're doing—with your teacher *and* with yourself.

➤ Remind yourself that your teacher is 100 percent human, just like you.

Your teacher is not larger than life, even if some of the folks around them think they are.

Once someone has learned to stay present and pay attention, they'll naturally notice things other folks don't. While we might call this a special talent, it's neither supernatural nor unique to spiritual teachers. Such people are just fully *here*, rather than lost in their thoughts or hopes or fears or agendas.

As a result, many spiritual teachers are especially good at listening, or observing, or empathizing, or intuiting what needs to be done. Others are especially good speakers, or writers, or one-to-one coaches.

It's also true that a small number of people do have unusual powers that 99 percent of us can never hope to replicate. Think of horse whisperers; people with photographic memories; folks who can instantly solve complex math problems in their heads; artists who can express the essence of an object in two or three brushstrokes; and folks who can look briefly at you and read your mind, or at least your emotional state. These seemingly larger-than-life powers are real but rare, and often inexplicable. Not that they need explaining.

Some special powers are downright trivial. The Zen teacher Joko Beck, who died in 2011, wrote that when she lived at the Zen Center of Los Angeles, she sometimes had the ability to see through the wall and discern what was being served for dinner in the dining hall two doors away. If it was something she didn't like, she wouldn't go. (As another spiritual teacher observed, "I'd call this the power of smelling and visualizing.")

I know a spiritual teacher who, for many years, had a knack for sensing people's energy—or, as some folks would put it, seeing their auras. He didn't talk about this a lot, but I watched him do it many times. As he approached middle age, that ability waned and then disappeared. Once it was gone, he told me he didn't miss it and that it probably did more harm than good.

Such special powers also appear to be randomly distributed. A spiritual teacher may be fortunate enough to have one of them—but so may a piano tuner, a bank teller, or a second-grade teacher. It's a mistake to equate these powers with spiritual insight. Sometimes they go together, but often they don't.

In practice, this means that someone who calls themselves a spiritual teacher may indeed have a special power of some kind—but this doesn't mean they're wise or loving. In fact, they may be a predator or charlatan who uses that power to impress, hoodwink, and then abuse their students.

Then there are those incidents where—for a moment—any of us may have seemingly superhuman insight. Something tells you to wait when the traffic signal turns green; a second later, a truck speeds through the intersection in front of you, its driver oblivious to the red light. Your stomach tightens whenever you talk to the friendly, gregarious man behind the bakery counter; then, one day, you see on the news that he's been arrested for sexually abusing his daughter. You say to a friend's son, "That job you just interviewed for—you're going to get it; I can feel it." You don't even know why you said it, but you turn out to be right. These incidents often defy our ability to explain them. Not that they need explaining, either.

Spiritual teachers sometimes have such moments of insight, just as many of us do. But that doesn't mean they're larger than life; it means that life is much larger than us.

Over time, your teacher will probably change the form or focus of what they teach.

Every decent spiritual teacher changes, grows, learns, and has new insights. Over time, this process naturally encourages them to alter how or what they teach.

This process includes making some mistakes or poor decisions. But if the teacher is honest and wise, they'll admit each error and make an appropriate adjustment. (If they can't or won't come clean about their mistakes, then they and their students are both headed for great suffering.)

Most spiritual teachers provide instruction in prayer, meditation, and/or other contemplative practices. Almost all students adopt these practices in the hope of becoming happier or calmer—but sometimes the short-term results are just the opposite.
When most of us take up any spiritual practice, we've already accumulated all kinds of ideas about it. Some of these ideas may get in our way; others are downright incorrect.

It's part of a spiritual teacher's job to instruct us in such practices—and, of course, to be very aware of their purposes and nuances. It's also part of their job to help us grow out of our misunderstandings about them.

For example, people often confuse meditation with trance states. They imagine that meditation takes us to a place outside of time and space, away from the present moment—a place beyond the worries, irritations, and terrors of life.

In fact, meditation is often precisely the opposite: full engagement *within* the here and now, and the acceptance of whatever arises. While meditation often leads to calmness, relaxation, and release, sometimes what shows up is worry, or irritation, or even terror. These may appear, swirl about for a time, and then drift off—without our having to direct or manage them. (If they appear regularly and don't go away, talk with your teacher about them.)

Prayer, too, can be easily misunderstood. Prayer can be an opening of the heart and a communion with the Divine. But a certain form of prayer can easily devolve into a kind of nagging—a recitation of a wish list or a plea to have our desires fulfilled. Later on, if we don't get what we ask for, we feel frustrated or angry. We wonder why our prayers weren't answered. But they are *always* answered. We just aren't happy when the answer is something other than *Here's everything you asked for.*

A similar dynamic can show up in our relationship with our spiritual teacher. We tell our teacher what we want—or what we think we need—and then expect them to provide it, as if they're a clerk in a department store. But a wise teacher will do what's in our best interests—which is not necessarily what we ask for or expect from them.

Authentic spiritual study and practices may lead to ecstasies, powerful body sensations, big insights—or none of the above.

Lots of experiences—meditation, yoga, prayer, chanting, sex, dancing, singing, working out, fasting, or taking mind-altering drugs—may generate bliss. Some may generate visions or hallucinations. Some can engender important insights. Some might generate a combination of the three.

But bliss, visions, and insights are three very different things—and we do ourselves a disservice by confusing them. While bliss is a common side effect of many spiritual practices, it is anything but the point of them.

Some people who claim to be on a spiritual path are actually bliss seekers, constantly chasing after a new, bigger, better buzz. They may frame this chase as a quest for a transcendent or transformative spiritual experience—but actually they just want to feel good. To these folks, activities such as visualizing angels, shooting energy up their spines, or feeling light radiate from their third eyes seem inherently spiritual. Meanwhile, they look at nurturing their kids, volunteering at a hospice, or delivering meals to elderly shut-ins as humdrum and ordinary. Yet which set of activities does our world need more?

Bliss seekers usually imagine that an important insight needs to be felt as a big shock to the body, like a surge of adrenaline or an orgasm. Sometimes that's the case, but not usually. More often there's just a sense of relief, because some long-standing confusion has cleared up. Sometimes there's no special bodily sensation at all.

Still, lots of people—even some spiritual teachers—equate a physical charge with religious insight. If they have an experience that shocks their body big time, they think it must be meaningful and important. I'm not saying their experience isn't real—just that there's nothing religious about it.

If you'd like to feel a big, exciting, full-body buzz, drink a double espresso, or try doing a dozen sun salutations. (The espresso is more reliable.) Either way, though, don't imagine that the buzz has anything to do with waking up.

Spiritual growth is rarely linear.

It's possible to build muscle or improve memory in a linear, incremental, step-by-step manner. But spiritual growth rarely works that way.

In fact, the very term *spiritual growth* is fraught with ambiguity. Although many people may speak of it, when you ask them to describe it or explain what it is, they aren't quite able to.

What we *can* do is grow up. We can become more patient, more open, more empathetic, more generous, more wise, more adult. We can see ourselves, our relationships, and the world more clearly. Through much success and failure, joy and disappointment, trial and error, we can become more human.

None of this takes place in a linear, measured, or quantified way.

Fortunately, there's no need to measure or quantify it. It's enough to simply experience it—and know in your body that it is real.

Relating to Your Teacher

Asking good questions is half of learning.

MUHAMMAD

It is one of the gifts of great spiritual teachers to make things simple. It is one of the gifts of their followers to complicate them again. Often we need to scrape away the accumulated complications of a master's message in order to hear the kernel of what they said.

JULIA CAMERON

The role of an effective teacher is to instruct, encourage, provide feedback, and inspire through personal example. Moreover, the more effective teachers tap and nurture the inherent potential of students, rather than imposing their own style and agenda.

JOHN WELWOOD

Once the seeker and the guide get to work, the seeker has to put some real weight on that trust in the guide rather quickly. He will be struggling to talk about deep and delicate things. She will be trying to express a hesitant but real desire to reach out to the transcendent Other with her whole heart. . . . A trustable guide will receive these men and women with transcendent respect and will not see them as only bundles of symptoms or a mere collection of sin and disorder. On the other hand, talking about sin and disorder will not be off limits. A trustworthy guide will (sometimes) be able to indicate what messages from the deeper self—and what bits of prudence from the revealed communal tradition—a man or woman may have been evading.

CAROLYN GRATTON

Feel free to bring your teacher any serious spiritual or religious question you may have— but you may not get a simple, straightforward, easy-to-comprehend answer.

We students often ask our spiritual teachers for a playbook for navigating life—as if life were static, predictable, or mechanical.

Sometimes we ask them for the secrets of the universe—as if truth were somewhere other than in plain view.

We ask them to put the ungraspable into graspable words and concepts.

We ask them to help us get a handle on the world—a world that *can't* be mastered, controlled, or boiled down into a set of instructions.

When we ask these things of our spiritual teachers, of course they don't give us the kind of answers we yearn for. They can't.

What a spiritual teacher *can* do is help us accept the pain and difficulty of life, and drop the delusion that it can be made into something other than what it is.

Even then, they can't wave their hands and magically unbind us from our delusion, as if we're helpless heroines tied to a railroad track. They can, however, help us see the ways in which we may indeed be bound up. They can raise questions about how and why we get into certain kinds of trouble, perhaps repeatedly. They can coach, encourage, and assist us in a variety of other ways. They can also model the way for living with presence, integrity, discernment, and compassion.

Our common habit is to ask our teachers subject-related questions and expect subject-related answers. But spiritual teachers often pay more attention to the state of mind—or the degree of awareness—from which our question emanates. They may then speak to that state rather than answer the literal question. As a result, what they say may sometimes surprise us, shock us, or pierce our heart.

Never be afraid to ask a teacher about something you don't understand.

Some of the most important words anyone can say to a spiritual teacher are, *I don't understand. Please help me.*

A wise and compassionate teacher will provide the kind of help you need in that moment. But that doesn't always mean leading you to cognitive clarity. Often it will mean pointing you in the right direction—or pulling you back from a potentially dangerous one.

When understanding does come, it may first show up in your body—in what you feel or do—and only later in your cognitive mind. Sometimes it may arrive in tandem with another question—or with distress or confusion. And sometimes it may sneak up on you, under your radar, and punch you in the gut.

When you face a difficult decision or situation, feel free to ask your teacher for advice.

It's fine to ask spiritual teachers for guidance or advice. But sometimes what we're really asking is for our teacher to be our surrogate parent and to tell us what to do. In essence, we say to them, *I want to be a child. Help me avoid the pain of making difficult decisions in an uncertain world. Make this decision for me.* The only sane answer to that request—and the only one that honors us and helps us grow up—is *no*.

Our teachers can—and often should—offer their advice. But no decent teacher will ask—or allow—us to give up our basic responsibilities as adult human beings. Even if we beg them to.

This is true even in spiritual traditions that include guru-disciple relationships. In these relationships, the guru is seen as a source of wisdom to which the disciple *voluntarily and provisionally* relinquishes their will in order to awaken, open, and grow. (We do something similar when we take a job and voluntarily and provisionally subordinate our will to the will of our boss.) But in all legitimate guru-disciple relationships—as well as most superior-subordinate ones—at all times both people remain adults who are responsible for their own actions and decisions. If our guru (or our boss) violates the boundaries of the relationship—for example, by ordering us to have sex with them—then it's our responsibility to say no, keep ourselves safe, and notify the proper authority.

In any healthy student-teacher relationship, each person is *always* responsible for what they say, do, and decide. Our teachers can guide us and encourage us. They can tell us when we're talking bullshit, or not thinking straight, or thinking too linearly or literally, or about to go off the rails. They can imagine themselves in our shoes. But they are— or at least should be—wise enough not to step into them.

In fact, if a spiritual teacher demands that you *mindlessly* obey or surrender to them—ostensibly as a way to release the bonds of your ego, or become more flexible or humble—run as fast as you can in the other direction. There's a good chance this teacher is a predator, a narcissist, or a charlatan.

But if the teacher talks about surrendering to the Divine or the Whole or the Absolute, rather than to *them personally*—or to some other human being—that's very different. *That* surrender can be essential to waking up.

Sometimes the best and most honest answer a spiritual teacher can give is, *I don't know.*
Our teachers don't—and can't—know everything about everything. (Anyone who claims that they do is either fraudulent or delusional.) But they can—and should—honestly admit when they're clueless about something. In fact, we all should.

At other times, your teacher's best and most honest answer might be, *That's none of my business.* And sometimes it might be, *I can't make your choice for you, but maybe I can help you with the process.* And occasionally it might be, *I'm clueless about this—but a good therapist (or physician or acupuncturist or lawyer) might be able to help.*

Feeling stuck or uncertain makes most of us uncomfortable. Our first impulse is to try to relieve that discomfort. But the discomfort is not what we need to resolve. In fact, it is often precisely *within* the discomfort where things can shift and a resolution can emerge.

Some teachers ask or encourage their students to make a formal commitment to spiritual study or practice. Others are much more informal, allowing each student to choose their own level of commitment and participation.

Like each musician, artist, or chef, each spiritual teacher has their own unique style and approach. Some are formal, others informal; some demanding, others flexible and easygoing.

Each student also comes to the student-teacher relationship with their own unique background, expectations, and illusions. Over time, a good spiritual teacher will recognize these and learn to work with (and sometimes around) them.

As their student, you also need to discern how to best work with (and sometimes around) your teacher's unique style, approach, and expectations.

And if the two of you simply don't work together well, you may need to find a different teacher. There's no shame in this; in fact, it's a part of many people's spiritual journeys.

Studying with some spiritual teachers feels much like taking an academic class. Other teachers create an environment similar to a literary salon. Still others require students to change into special clothes, do specific spiritual practices, and follow a formal routine. All of these variations are potentially legitimate; all can be helpful; and all have their drawbacks and dangers.

In an open society, there will always be a wide range of spiritual forms—and an even wider array of teachers—to choose from. As students, each of us must use our discernment to find a wise and compassionate teacher, as well as a form (and, usually, a tradition) that resonates deeply with us.

In one sense, the form is not terribly important, since the water of wisdom flows into vessels of many different shapes and colors. But in another sense, form *is* important, because not all of us can see every color, or drink readily from vessels of every size and shape. Each of us needs to choose a form that works for us and feels right—without becoming beholden to it, or believing it's the one and only form for everyone, or forbidding ourselves to explore any alternatives.

It's also true that poison can flow just as easily into many different kinds of vessels. This is why it's so important to move slowly and carefully in building a relationship with any spiritual teacher, to repeatedly question and test them; to trust your

own intuition and insights; and to disengage, sometimes quickly, when you realize that you've made a
mistake.

Wisdom takes many forms. So do ignorance,
deceit, and mental illness.

**There's no point in trying to impress your
teacher or win their approval.**

Moreover, with an authentic teacher, it's not going to
work. Any spiritual teacher worth their salt will be
unmoved—or even mildly annoyed—by attempts to
suck up to them. They've accepted the teacher role in
order to help others grow up. And no one matures
through ass-kissing; we mature through experience
and service.

If a teacher does respond positively to flattery or
brownnosing—or, worse, if they encourage it—take
this as a huge red flag.

**Emulating your teacher's habits, mannerisms,
lifestyle, or way of speaking probably won't
improve your life or make you more spiritual.
It may even make your life smaller.**

Spiritual teachers can serve as our role models for
important things such as empathy, patience, compassion, presence, and a spirit of service. In these

aspects of life, we would be wise to observe them and follow their lead.

Some students, however, miss this point and instead mimic trivial details. They habitually repeat some of the things their teachers say, or wear similar clothing, or eat the same foods. They imagine that by imitating these details, they can acquire (or pretend to exhibit) spiritual wisdom. This is misguided at best, foolish and boorish at worst. Any legitimate spiritual teacher wants to nurture insight, not train parrots or recruit a band of clones.

As children, we emulated the adults around us, trying on their habits and mannerisms to see how well they suited us. This was normal—and useful— behavior for us as kids.

But then we grew up. As part of that maturing, we learned not to mindlessly follow in others' footsteps, but to step forward on our own. A relationship with any spiritual teacher should support and encourage this process, not undermine it.

Any authentic religious practice helps us to grow into ourselves—not into a mold shaped like someone else.

In order to be as helpful as they can, your teacher may ask you some personal questions. This is both normal and appropriate. Nevertheless, you don't have to give your teacher any information that you're uncomfortable revealing.

It's not unusual for a spiritual teacher to probe, challenge, or ask questions. Some of these questions might seem rude or invasive if they were to come from a stranger—or a less-than-close friend.

It's also not unusual for discussions between students and spiritual teachers to delve into some intimate topics. In these discussions, it's the teacher's duty to set aside their own agenda and desires, and to do whatever is in the student's best interests.

All of this is the opposite of a teacher—or anyone—violating your personal boundaries for their own purposes. If that happens, you'll probably feel it in your body—perhaps as an unease, or a tightening, or a recoiling, or outright fear. Pay attention to such feelings, and take their arising very seriously. Tell the person they need to stop or back off. If they don't, question or confront them—or simply leave.

At times, you may feel strong emotions toward your teacher—sometimes many different ones in quick succession, or even all at once.
Typically, these include gratitude, awe, anger, attraction, envy, shock, disgust, disappointment, infatuation, adoration, and love. Most of the time these feelings will reflect you, not your teacher.

A good spiritual teacher will act as a mirror, helping you to look at your own mind, your interactions with other people, and your relationship with the world.

It's quite common—especially in the early stages of a student-teacher relationship—for us to project all kinds of things onto our teachers: our hopes, fears, desires, ideals, and/or authority issues. We may also project onto them the ability to fulfill or heal us—as if they can somehow do our own internal work for us.

Psychotherapists call such projections—the transferring of our past emotions onto someone in the present—*transference.* Transference keeps us from seeing our teachers as they are; instead, we see them through our own past and projections.

This is common, and it's even normal—but we also need to recognize it and work to grow out of it.

A good teacher will recognize it as well—and work around it, call it out, and/or help you work through it.

Your relationship with your teacher will change over time.

This is because *every* important relationship in your life will change over time.

You will change as well—perhaps dramatically— as you age and experience new circumstances and events.

Relationships with spiritual teachers tend to change over time for another reason: as we let go of our projections, assumptions, and illusions about them, we see them for who they actually are. This can take years—sometimes decades. But when it does occur, it provides a great opportunity for learning and waking up.

Every six months, step back and take a look at yourself, your teacher, your relationship with them, and your life as a whole.

The human brain constantly looks for shortcuts— ways to think and act and be that don't require our full discernment and presence. When we find one that seems to work fairly well, we tend to use it as a substitute for engagement with the here and now. Sometimes this works fine, but often it can lead to trouble.

Every moment of our lives is new, fresh, and unique. It's also an opportunity—and a call, and a challenge—to be awake, alert, and present to what's going on. Then we need to act on a case-by-case, moment-by-moment basis, with as much discernment as we can. Working with a good spiritual teacher helps us lean into this awake, responsible, discerning way of living.

Taking stock of any important relationship—and your life as a whole—enables you to bring this discernment to some of the larger arcs in your life. It also helps you see where you've replaced your full presence with shortcuts.

Here are some helpful questions to ask yourself:

> *What's working? What's not?*

> *What do I keep? What do I let go of?*

> *What changes do I want to make?*

> *What changes do I need to make?*

> *What changes are unavoidable, and how can I adjust to them?*

➢ *What feels right? What feels wrong?*

➢ *What am I taking for granted?*

This kind of periodic review of your relationship with your teacher—done privately, in your own mind and heart, in a setting where you can be free of distraction—can help you make the most of that relationship. It might also lead to a valuable discussion with your teacher.

Or, sometimes, it may help you recognize that it's wise to end the relationship and find a different teacher.

Is there ever a time when you can let go of these occasional reflections? I would say no. Your teacher will change. You will change. Your relationship will change. The world will change. But your need for discernment, examination, and presence never ends.

No matter what your teacher says, does, or asks of you, your decisions and actions are your own responsibility.

No matter what *anyone* says, does, or asks of you, your decisions and actions are your own responsibility. It's an unavoidable part of the human condition.

Trying to abdicate this responsibility to someone else—a partner, a parent, a leader, or a spiritual teacher—makes life more difficult for both of you.

More notably, it doesn't work. You can't outsource your own important decisions any more than you can have someone else eat or breathe for you.

Furthermore, even if you do try to give away your authority, *you're* the one choosing to divest yourself of it—which continues to make you responsible.

4

Red Flags and Warning Signs

No person is your friend who demands your silence, or denies your right to grow.

ALICE WALKER

A true teacher won't try to sell you anything or convince you of anything. . . . They won't use a lot of gimmicks and gadgetry to try to entice you, either. Nor will they have any interest in controlling or manipulating you in any way. . . . A true teacher doesn't want you to worship them or to come to them for guidance, as if their job is to steer your life. . . . A good teacher will not put you in a position where you need to rely on them. . . . Similarly, a good teacher won't need you.

They won't need (or expect) you to stay with them, and they won't be personally invested in what you do or the choices you make. A true teacher won't try to make you into something you're not, especially not a trophy or plaything of their own.

STEVE HAGEN

If everything has to be perfect, and positive, and anything less is banished, watch out. . . . Where someone else's ground rules supersede yours, be alert. . . . If people spend a lot of time rationalizing, reframing or denying the leader's inconsistent or unkind behavior, pay attention.

ALISON ROSE LEVY

Be sure to examine the teacher's other students. Do they look healthy and radiant or haggard and under-nourished? Do they seem balanced and genuine or unbalanced and contrived? Pay attention to any vague discomfort you might feel in the presence of some teachers and their communities. These feelings could be a keen intuition that something is amiss.

GREG BOGART

If a spiritual teacher is bogus or dangerous, they'll provide plenty of warning signs.
Something is potentially fishy if a teacher does one or more of the following—especially repeatedly:

- ➤ Claims they have the Answer and can give it to you.

- ➤ Doesn't practice what they preach.

- ➤ Claims that the normal rules or codes of conduct don't apply to them.

- ➤ Claims to be all-knowing or infallible.

- ➤ Acts superior to others, or is routinely rude or dismissive to them.

- ➤ Pressures (rather than welcomes) people to study with them or join their spiritual community.

- ➤ Has (or tries to have) sex with their students.

- ➤ Acts in a way that harms others, then claims it's "crazy wisdom," or "skillful means," or "the left-handed path," or part of their training or tradition.

- ➤ Publicly shames or demeans some of their students.

- ➤ Uses lots of words and phrases that only they and their students understand.

- ➤ Encourages all their students to talk, act, or think the same way.

- ➤ Doesn't say, "I made a mistake," "I stand corrected," or "I was wrong."

- ➤ Acts very holy, or conspicuously calm or serene, in public.

- ➤ Demands strict obedience and/or veneration.

- ➤ Discourages visits and inquiry from people outside their group.

- ➤ Discourages people from examining or questioning what they say, and asks them to take it purely on faith.

- ➤ Encourages people to do something that's physically damaging or dangerous—or, worse, *demands* that they do it.

- ➤ Wants (or demands) things from their students— obedience, money, veneration, gifts, flattery, etc.

➤ Keeps information secret that should normally be made public (e.g., mistakes they have made, or the finances of their organization).

➤ Reveals information that should normally be kept private (e.g., confidential personal details revealed to them by their students).

➤ Has a tribal view of the world, in which members of their group or religion are pitted against outsiders.

➤ Charges money for anything and everything they do.

➤ Charges unusually high fees.

➤ Exerts heavy pressure on you to make contributions of time or money, especially large ones.

➤ Adopts a public face that contradicts how they behave in private.

➤ Seems to be trying to build a spiritual empire.

➤ Purports to be something other than a normal flesh-and-blood human being.

Consider each of these a big red flag. And when multiple red flags get raised and waved, protect yourself by getting away.

If a spiritual teacher does act in one or more of these ways, they (and their followers) will usually have an elaborate justification for it. Trust your own intuition and discernment, not the justification.

At the heart of every healthy student-teacher relationship are four essential elements.

1. The student's desire to become wiser or more fully human.

2. The teacher's commitment (either overt or implied) to assist the student in that endeavor.

3. The teacher's commitment to consistently act in the student's best interests. This includes not harming or exploiting the student in any way.

4. The student's honest intention to not exploit the teacher for gratification or gain.

At the heart of most *unhealthy* student-teacher relationships is the teacher's failure to honor one or more of their commitments.

The great majority of spiritual teachers put their students' interests ahead of their own. But there are some very notable exceptions—and we need to be alert for them.

Sadly, it can be easier for a predator, narcissist, or person with serious delusions to be a spiritual teacher than to be a competent electrician, librarian, or line cook. Indeed, the role of spiritual teacher is almost perfectly designed to attract those types of people.

Consider what being a spiritual teacher usually means. People look up to you (though they really shouldn't). Some revere or adore you. Many believe you're special. They trust you with their most intimate emotions, often with their secrets, and sometimes with their money. They sit in rapt attention, taking in your every word. Some will gladly follow your orders. Some will throw themselves at your feet if you let them. Some will climb into bed with you if you ask. For someone with delusions of grandeur, being a spiritual teacher is an ideal role. For a predator, it provides a community populated with many easy marks.

Furthermore, there aren't a lot of obvious reality checks for people who call themselves spiritual teachers. If someone says, "I'm a wise and special hair stylist," then we expect them to do amazing things with hair. If they claim to be a world-class mechanic, then they have to demonstrate a special talent for repairing cars. If, in either case, they can't, then it's obvious to everyone that they're either fraudulent or deluded.

But most people can't easily judge whether someone is a decent spiritual teacher. Most people evaluate teachers by their charisma, or their cleverness, or their fame, or the number of students or followers they have, or the amount of publicity they get, or the number of books they write and sell. But none of these measuring sticks is remotely relevant. In fact, narcissists tend to be exceptionally charismatic—and extremely good at getting people to follow them. The same is true of many sociopaths.

Most of us assume that wisdom and sanity automatically go together. Often they do. But not always. It's quite possible to have a good deal of spiritual insight and, at the same time, a mental illness. It's also possible to convincingly fake that insight by mimicking others who do have it.

This doesn't mean you should be wary of all spiritual teachers. Do, however, proceed slowly and carefully, just as you would with any other important relationship. Take things one step at a time. Be willing to pause and take stock. Catch your breath and process what you've experienced. Pay attention to what your body, heart, and head tell you. If they're not aligned, take this as an important yellow flag. Observe the teacher some more. Observe your own responses further as well. Maybe even go away for a while. Then, if it feels right, wade in again—deeper this time. It's exactly what you'd do with a new doctor, or counselor, or romantic partner.

Pay attention to your body and your intuition for warnings. If something doesn't feel or look or sound right, it probably isn't. It doesn't matter if everyone else around you believes in the teacher, and thinks they're great, and is following them enthusiastically. If your own internal alarm goes off, listen to it. Ask questions. Challenge people. If your alarm keeps ringing, get up and leave.

Also use the internet. If you're interested in a particular spiritual teacher, Google them. Or you might Google their name and *scandal*, or their name and *sociopath*, or their name and *narcissist*. If multiple people say similar negative things about a teacher, take their comments seriously. Watch for patterns.

The best and simplest rule of thumb may be this: if a teacher is inherently exploitive or abusive, they'll want something from you. Often it's sex. Sometimes it's money—usually lots of it. Almost always, it's power over you. Often it's your loyalty or adoration.

At the beginning of this chapter, I provided a list of red flags and warning signs. In his wonderfully sane and observant article "Early Warning Signs for the Detection of Spiritual Blight," Daniel Goleman provides his own pithy, parallel list of such signs. That list is worth excerpting here:

> *Taboo topics:* Questions that can't be asked, doubts that can't be shared, misgivings that can't be voiced . . .

> *Spiritual Clones:* An entire group of people who manifest only a narrow range of feeling . . .

> *Groupthink:* A party line that overrides how people actually feel . . .

> *The Elect:* A shared delusion of grandeur that there is no Way but this one . . .

> *No Graduates:* Members are never weaned from the group . . .

> *Assembly Lines:* Everyone is treated identically, no matter what their differences . . .

➤ *Loyalty Tests:* Members are asked to prove loyalty to the group by doing something that violates their personal ethics . . .

➤ *Duplicity:* The group's public face misrepresents its true nature . . .

➤ *Unifocal Understanding:* A single worldview is used to explain anything and everything; alternate explanations are verboten . . .

➤ *Humorlessness:* No irreverence allowed.

And if you want a good laugh as well as a further wake-up call, Google "The Trickster Guru," Alan Watts's snarky but wise essay on fraudulent spiritual teachers. (Watts was a brilliant writer, but he himself was not a spiritual role model. He referred to himself—accurately—as a "philosophical entertainer" and a "genuine fake.")

One final thought: the more famous and revered a teacher is, the more careful I encourage you to be. A small but significant percentage of our most lauded spiritual teachers are narcissists and sociopaths in disguise. I've seen this over and over—and written about it extensively in my book *Sex and the Spiritual Teacher.*

If you think a teacher may be slowly and subtly—or not so slowly or subtly—attempting to seduce you, it's unlikely that it's all in your imagination. We students often find spiritual teachers inherently seductive. Partly it's because they're leaders, authority figures, and role models; partly it's because of the wisdom they have (or purport to have). On top of this, many spiritual teachers are charismatic—or at least some combination of eloquent, smart, and funny. It's only natural to like them, want them to like us, and want to be close (or special) to them.

There's more. A spiritual teacher typically develops great spiritual intimacy and connection with their students. That's why it sometimes looks like they can read our minds. (And, in some cases, maybe they can.)

Add these together, and it's no surprise that many students feel a strong energetic pull toward their teachers. Often this pull is partly experienced as sexual, particularly among people in their twenties and thirties.

If a teacher is good looking, that adds even more sexual energy to the dynamic. And if the teacher is married or partnered or celibate, for some students the forbidden-fruit factor turns up the heat even more.

Spiritual teachers are keenly aware of this, of course—and the honorable ones simply allow the sexual energy to bounce off them.

Unfortunately, some spiritual teachers respond to that energy. Some do it overtly, some subtly and incrementally. Their response can show up as favoritism or praise. It can be a lingering look or touch. It can be purely energetic—i.e., the teacher holds all the usual boundaries in place and doesn't give the student any special look or touch or treatment, but they blast the student with sexual energy.

If you get the sense that your spiritual teacher is sexually or romantically interested in you, notice what you feel in your body. Then step back for a time. You may need to disengage from the teacher and your spiritual community for a week or two, and see how that feels. When you're outside the swirl of energy, you can assess your situation more honestly and accurately.

That said, it's also possible to err in the other direction, by mistaking a teacher's genuine warmth, insight, and openness for a special kind of interest in you personally.

You need to use your powers of discernment— both your cognitive skills and your intuition—in any important relationship. This is doubly important for a relationship with a spiritual teacher.

It's equally important to build such a relationship slowly, carefully, and incrementally, so that any decision you make, or conclusion you come to, is informed by plenty of firsthand experience.

If you come to the conclusion that your teacher is sexually or romantically interested in you, then you have some tough decisions to make.
You may need to bluntly raise the issue with the teacher—and perhaps set a clear boundary. For instance: "I don't want you to be my lover. I want you for my teacher—and nothing more." Or, "I'm not having sex with you. Period." Or, "I'm flattered, but I'm not interested." (Don't be surprised if your relationship with your teacher becomes different as a result. If it does, recognize that the change is your teacher's doing, because they're the one who brought the possibility of sex into it.)

You're almost certainly headed for trouble if you just go with the flow. You'll allow yourself to be lured into bed—or will jump into it willingly. Then you'll have to try to figure out what to do next.

Sexual interest in a spiritual teacher can lead students in many directions. In very rare cases, it has led to a lifetime of monogamous happiness. Much more often, it leads to a single quick sexual encounter on the teacher's desk or kitchen table, after which the teacher withdraws their interest and acts like the sex never happened. It can lead to an attempt by the teacher to dominate the student's life, actions, and thoughts. It can also lead to betrayal, a broken marriage, emotional trauma, and an STD. In short, it's just like any other relationship entered into thoughtlessly or hastily.

When a spiritual teacher is dishonorable and exploitive, there's an added twist. They are deeply familiar with the workings of the human psyche—so if their motives are selfish, they can be a master manipulator.

It's fine for a spiritual teacher to be wealthy if they earned or inherited their money—but if their wealth comes from their students, consider this a huge warning sign.

Many well-known religious figures have either a lot of money or none at all. On the one hand there are the saints and the monastics and the renunciates, who rarely even handle money. Then there are the ministers of megachurches and the writers of spiritual bestsellers, who make millions. There are also, of course, plenty of folks in between.

How lavishly a teacher lives isn't necessarily important. But what *is* deeply important is where their money came from.

If a teacher is wealthy because of earnings from legitimate investments or an honorable business, or if they inherited it, or if they wrote a wise and helpful book that sold a lot of copies, that's fine. But if their money comes primarily from their students— whether it's course fees, or donations they encouraged, or free will offerings—then wealth or a lavish lifestyle is completely unjustified.

We all need—and deserve—to eat. We also deserve to be free from exploitation.

Spiritual guidance is not a product to be delivered at the highest cost that the market will bear. It's a form of love and service. As such, it should either be given freely or—when circumstances warrant— provided at a fair and affordable price.

If you see a teacher living large off the backs of their students, turn around and run.

The most common error sincere spiritual teachers make is believing themselves to be wiser or more aware than they actually are.

Mariana Caplan has written an extremely valuable book on this subject, *Halfway Up the Mountain: The Error of Premature Claims to Enlightenment*, which I strongly recommend.

Because this error is so common, there's never a time when our own powers of discernment—our cognitive skills, our intuition, and our courage to question and investigate—become optional. We always need them, even with the people we trust the most. This is not because human beings are inherently malicious or selfish, but because all of us are fallible. No one is exempt from this reality—including spiritual teachers.

We're also all subject to change. There's no such thing as a fixed personality. None of us is the same person as we were a year or a decade (or, in truth, a minute) ago. Events change us. Insights change us.

Biology changes us, too. So does time. Three of my closest friends—all of them sane, smart, and astute—developed serious mental illnesses in middle age. The cause was genetics: each had a parent who had suffered a similar emotional takedown. As my friends aged, the illnesses embedded in their genes emerged.

About a decade ago, I met a highly respected spiritual teacher who came down with dementia as she grew old. She continued to teach, but her decisions and actions became steadily more questionable. Her neurological decline overshadowed her very real wisdom.

We need to accept the sad and humbling fact that even the wisest spiritual teacher can't pray or meditate away their DNA.

5

The Off-Duty Spiritual Teacher

I don't want to be in the role of "wisdom guy" all the time. I like it when I do it, but all the time? I mean, who wants to sit around talking about the Truth for any longer than is absolutely necessary?

ADYASHANTI

Part of developing healthy boundaries involves being clear about your public and your private space. When are you available or "on duty," and when are you "off duty"? Some students can feel that we teachers are available all of the time. Often we do work more unsociable hours such as evenings and weekends, but that does not mean that we have to be available all of the time.

DEE APOLLINE

Everyone's looking for the perfect teacher, but although their teachings might be divine, teachers are all too human, and that's something people find hard to accept.

DIEDRE O'NEILL, FROM PAULO COELHO'S NOVEL
THE WITCH OF PORTOBELLO

Roshi's favorite place to eat out was The Embers on Hennepin Avenue. The Embers was a chain restaurant like Denny's. Who in our hip natural-foods, macrobiotic generation wanted to eat there? Once, when my friend Kate and I ate dinner at their apartment above the zendo, Roshi asked us if we wanted wine. Yes, we said. He brought out a gallon box—not even a bottle—of Gallo . . .

NATALIE GOLDBERG,
FROM HER MEMOIR *LONG QUIET HIGHWAY*

Your teacher's off-duty life is probably different from what you imagine it to be. For the most part, it's also none of your business.

You should of course expect your teacher to live a sane, compassionate, and ethical life. It they don't, then studying with them may bring more suffering than wisdom into your life. Indeed, they probably shouldn't be a spiritual teacher in the first place.

Otherwise, though, let your teacher be different from you. Also let them be eccentric.

Your teacher probably has some hobbies, tastes, or interests that you don't share or appreciate. So long as these do no harm, don't evaluate the teacher by them. Truth is in plain sight, available to everyone—which means that some of the folks who can point out truth to us will have tastes and habits that baffle (or even offend) us.

Collectively, some of the spiritual teachers I know have regularly eaten sprouts, gyoza, Dairy Queen, and the salad bar at Friendly's; paid to see the films *The Tempest*, *Babe*, and *Nightmare on Elm Street 3*; enjoyed Wittgenstein, Dickens, comic books, and *Weirdo* magazine; listened regularly to Sibelius, Schoenberg, rock 'n' roll, and Rush Limbaugh; and driven a Prius, a station wagon, a beat-up Corolla, a bright red Celica, and a Porsche.

Your teacher is not free of normal human problems and dilemmas—e.g., reckless drivers, annoying neighbors, crazy relatives, or difficult personal decisions.

Spiritual insight is not a form of magic. It does not protect anyone—including our teachers, or us— from the inevitable storms of life.

Such insight can, however, help our teachers— and us—stay present and grounded, and be less tossed about when storms do blow through. It can help us discern what is actually going on, as opposed to what we hope or fear is happening. It can also help us to watch our own minds.

Perhaps most important, it can help us avoid worsening the situation by picking a fight, throwing a fit, standing pointlessly on a principle, staying quiet when speaking up is necessary, speaking up when silence is wiser, doing nothing when mindful action is called for, or doing something when doing nothing is the best (or least damaging) option.

If you see your teacher when they're off duty, don't expect them to automatically take on their teaching role—and don't assume that what they say or do is intended as instruction.
We shouldn't expect a spiritual teacher to be on duty 24/7. They get to have a life. And they get to say to us, "Not now; I'm off duty," as well as, "I'd like some privacy, please."

Yet it's also true that there's never a time when a spiritual teacher is off duty as a role model. We can and should expect them to live an admirable, compassionate, and ethical life—whether they're on duty or off.

We shouldn't require our spiritual teachers to be perfect—or to never have bad days. But even on their bad days—when they might be exhausted or grumpy or overwhelmed—we *should* still expect them to be compassionate and ethical, just as we would expect a therapist or a judge to be.

If a spiritual teacher waxes eloquent on unflappable patience and calmness but often throws a fit with their own teenagers, we can (correctly) consider them a hypocrite. The same is true for any spiritual teacher who holds their students to a higher ethical standard than they hold themselves. Indeed, the real test of anyone's ethics is how they act under difficult, painful circumstances.

Some FAQs

6

You can tell whether a man is wise by his questions.

NAGUIB MAHFOUZ

Questions can be like a lever you use to pry open the stuck lid on a paint can.

FRAN PEAVEY

The important thing is not to stop questioning. . . . Never lose a holy curiosity.

ALBERT EINSTEIN

Question everything.

ATTRIBUTED TO SOCRATES,
EURIPEDES, DESCARTES,
AND NEIL DEGRASSE TYSON

**Can the leader of my church or congrega-
tion—my minister or priest or rabbi or imam or
sensei—also be my spiritual teacher?**

Yes, but with some caveats.

First, both of you have to fully understand and
agree to your roles. You need to make it clear to your
spiritual leader that you want their close and ongoing spiritual guidance. They need to make it equally
clear to you that they're willing to take on that role.

The two of you also have to work out the details
of the relationship. Are they available for counseling
on a regular basis? As needed but by appointment?
On demand? They need to set clear boundaries
about what they will and won't do for you, and what
you should and shouldn't expect of them.

The arrangement also has to be 100 percent
mutual—and built on mutual respect. Both of you
need to share the same goal: to help you to grow up
and grow wiser.

It's also important to keep in mind that your
spiritual leader will have a unique relationship with
each congregant. Father Michael might have a con-
gregation of 140, and 10 of them might consider him
their spiritual teacher—but the other 130 may see
him as simply the parish priest.

How do I ask someone to be my spiritual teacher?

Some traditions and teachers have a clear, formal, official process. If this applies in your case, simply follow protocol.

If there's no formal process in place, there's nothing wrong with bluntly saying, "I'd like to be your student." But if the teacher says, "no," or "not now," or "maybe later; we'll see," accept their answer graciously.

That doesn't mean you have to slink away and disappear; presumably you can still listen to their talks, attend some of their public events, read their books, watch their videos, and so on.

If the teacher does say yes, it's critical that the two of you get clear about what your relationship will entail. Otherwise, at least one of you may feel disappointed, confused, or even betrayed.

Once I become someone's student, what are their obligations to me? What are my obligations to them? And what are my obligations to myself?

First and foremost, each of you needs to treat the other with respect.

Second, each of you needs to treat *yourself* with respect.

Third, each of you needs to be as honest as you can—with yourself and with each other. You each need to avoid—and, if necessary, note—any manipulation, flattery, or attempts to win the other's approval or praise.

Fourth, don't ask or expect your teacher to do the impossible—or the needlessly difficult. They won't be available to you whenever you want them to be. They won't remove your pain or confusion for you—though they can support and encourage you as you work through them. And they can't protect you from the slings and arrows of life.

Fifth, don't ask them for answers to questions that are outside their purview and experience. Spiritual insight doesn't make someone an expert in investing, or nutrition, or auto repair, or child rearing.

Lastly, and most importantly, your teacher needs to *always* act in your best interests. If and when they see that *you're* not acting in your own best interests, they need to call you on it, as wisely and compassionately as they can.

Sometimes this may involve what's called *skillful means* or *crazy wisdom*—some temporary misdirection or misinformation to help you wake up. Think of it as a metaphorical—but *never* an actual—whack on the side of the head. If that metaphorical whacking doesn't work, however, and you don't recognize the intended purpose behind it, the teacher needs to quickly come clean about what they did and why.

Now let's turn this around. If there ever comes a time when you suspect that your teacher *isn't* acting in your best interests, you need to call *them* on it, as wisely and compassionately as you can.

It's unlikely but possible that the teacher will respond by saying, "I *am* acting in your best interests. I know what's best for you, and you don't. Now do what I say, not what feels right and honest and loving." If you have the misfortune of being told this, find the nearest exit and quickly flee.

Is it okay to have more than one spiritual teacher at a time?

The simple answer is yes. After all, wisdom doesn't reside in any one person or tradition.

But a student-teacher relationship *can* be quite spiritually intimate. As a result, over time you may decide to make someone your primary (or sole) teacher. While this isn't required, most students find themselves doing this eventually.

You might make this commitment overtly, through an agreement with your teacher (and, in some traditions, perhaps with a ceremony). Or you might simply recognize the nature of the relationship in your own heart and mind.

If you don't eventually choose a primary teacher, it's worth looking at your mind and motives. If you play one teacher against the other, or teacher-hop until you find someone who tells you exactly what you want to hear, then you're shooting yourself in the foot. You'd be better off sticking with one teacher whom you trust, who will speak the truth to you, and who will insist that you speak the truth to yourself.

That said, any spiritual teacher gets to have their own opinion about other teachers. Teacher A may recommend that you also study with Teacher B— and perhaps avoid Teacher C. It's up to you to discern and decide how much of this advice to follow. But if a spiritual teacher *forbids* you to work with *any* other teacher, consider this a giant red flag.

When I meet a teacher who's being venerated or toadied to, how can I act so that I neither buy into the veneration nor step on anyone's toes?

If there's a ritual everyone else is following—bowing, or chanting, or praying, or whatever—follow the basics of the form, so you don't disturb people or get in the way. Do this out of simple respect and politeness, in the same way that you'd remove your hat in a theater so the person behind you can see.

But you don't have to fully participate. If someone tries to hand you a bowl of rose petals and says, "Toss these on guru-ji's path," you can smile and say, "No, thank you. I'm a visitor here. Please give the honor to someone else." Or simply walk to the back of the group, where you'll be out of the way.

At the same time, observe your own emotional response—without necessarily expressing it. Let it flow into you—and then let go of it. Don't wallow in it, no matter what's going on around you. Stay present and alert to what's happening, both outside and inside you.

If you think you might act badly, simply leave. (This is good advice for any situation where you might do something you'll later regret.)

Afterward, if you like, ask the teacher or a senior student questions about the ritual.

Is it okay to ask a spiritual teacher if they're enlightened or fully awake?

People often wonder if they can ask teachers to describe their own awakenings—or if these are considered deeply personal questions, like asking someone to talk about losing their virginity.

There's nothing wrong with asking about someone's awakening. But how, where, and when you ask makes a difference.

You'd normally ask a surgeon questions about an upcoming operation when you first meet them in their office—not in the operating room, just before you're about to go under their knife. And it would be insulting to say to them, "Are you a great surgeon or just an average one?"

But there are some much bigger concerns here. Let's walk through each of them.

First, there's the question of what you mean by *enlightened* or *fully awakened*. Those terms get tossed around a lot, and some people use them in a way that's vague and almost meaningless.

A better question might be, *Do you have deep spiritual insight, or are you an ordinary person who is able to lead and guide others?* Many authentic, principled teachers will answer, "Both." (Most exploitive teachers will tell you that they're quite special.)

If what you want to know is, *Have you had a big, profound, sudden realization—what the Japanese Zen folks call* kensho?; *if so, please tell me about it*, then ask that.

But keep in mind that it's possible to wake up without having a big, singular experience. Some teachers' wisdom grows slowly and steadily, year by year. Their realizations are ripples and waves—not tsunamis.

Many people think that enlightenment is like getting a tattoo—i.e., once wisdom appears, it stays with you for the rest of your life. In some cases, that's true. But many other teachers lose their wisdom—and, sometimes, their way—over time. I've watched some stumble and recover, and others stumble, fall, and never get up.

There's also the issue of certification and endorsement. Perhaps what you're really concerned about is whether a teacher has received formal validation from their own teacher or spiritual tradition—as well as some guidance or instruction in how to teach. It's fine to ask this—but be explicit about it. For example: *I'm curious about your training and your authorization to teach. When, how, and from whom did you receive that authorization?*

Authorization—from a board, a school, or another teacher—is a double-edged sword. On the one hand, the lack of such authorization means that the spiritual teacher is self-proclaimed. It's important to approach any such teacher with caution and skepticism at first. Observe them for some months before you begin to build a one-to-one relationship with them.

On the other hand, a formal authorization is no guarantee that the authorizing person or group was wise in conferring it. There's a long and unfortunate tradition of spiritual teachers giving full endorsement to their partners or kids. This is fine when the partners and kids genuinely have the requisite insight—and a strong ability to lead and teach. But often they don't.

All of this means that there's never a time when you can—or should—stop relying on your own discernment.

Here's another twist. Sometimes when a student asks a teacher "Are you enlightened?" the student is actually looking for a reason to slack off. They think, *My teacher had a profound awakening, and they've been certified and endorsed by their own teacher. That means I can take on faith whatever they say. I don't have to be present. I don't have to be discerning. I don't have to ask probing questions. I don't have to consider what they say carefully and test it against my own experience and observation. I can just do what they say or follow their lead.* That's exactly when the student stops growing up. When a good teacher sees a student doing this, they'll call the student on it.

One more observation: when a teacher answers questions about their own awakening, they may or may not give you the kind of answer you expect. A lot depends on the context. Did you ask the question after the teacher has given a talk or presentation to a general audience? During the fifth day of a retreat? As part of a one-to-one meeting with the them?

The teacher's response might also depend on what they sense about your motivation or state of mind. They may recognize another, deeper inquiry behind the question you've asked—and speak to that inquiry instead.

What's the etiquette for questioning or challenging a spiritual teacher?

Challenging and asking questions—of our teachers and of ourselves—is at the center of spiritual life.

Any teacher who's even partly awake will welcome and encourage questions. Indeed, questioning and challenging are essential to growing up—and waking up.

That said, it's important to look at your motivation for asking a question or issuing a challenge. If your purpose is to clear up your own confusion, then just about any straightforward question or respectful challenge is fair game. (Though you'll need to discern whether it's best to ask the question publicly—for example, after a lecture—or privately, in a one-to-one conversation with the teacher.)

But if your main motivation is to show off your own insight or knowledge, or to try to debunk or embarrass the teacher, it's usually better to stay silent.

If you *are* genuinely seeking clarity, frame your question in terms of your confusion. Say, "Help me understand . . ." or "I'm confused about . . ." or "Would you clarify what you said about . . ." or "What you said about _____ doesn't make sense to me; can you say more?"

You can frame a direct challenge in a similar way. For example, "What you said about peak experiences seems to contradict what experimental psychologists have recently learned. Can you resolve this apparent contradiction for me?'"

If you have an important question for your teacher that, for whatever reason, you're afraid to ask, acknowledge your fear and ask the question anyway. (But pick a time and a situation that are appropriate—for you, the teacher, and the community.) It's very likely that other people have the same question, but haven't asked it because of fears of their own.

Is it okay to be friends with your spiritual teacher, or are the two roles incompatible?
It's always fine to be friendly with your teacher. It's also usually fine to occasionally do something social together. But being intimate friends, as well as student and teacher, is potentially dicey. And complicated.

If you feel that a serious friendship with your teacher is starting to develop—or if you'd like to see one develop—talk to your teacher about it, honestly and directly.

Don't be surprised if they disappoint you by saying, "You can be my student or my friend, but not both"—or, more simply, "Please just be my student." Because of the potential for role confusion, conflict, and eventual regret that such a dual relationship can create, the teacher may feel that a boundary needs to be set or that a choice needs to be made.

Is there any circumstance in which it's okay for me to get romantically or sexually involved with my spiritual teacher?

If you're someone's student, it's almost always unwise to begin a romantic or sexual relationship with them. This is the case regardless of who initiates it, how strongly the two of you feel about each other, and how unique the two of you feel your situation is. (This sense of uniqueness is actually surprisingly common.) It's a potential recipe for great conflict, enormous role confusion, and emotional pain galore.

The conflict and pain won't just be felt by the two of you. It will likely permeate your whole spiritual community. And that's assuming the two of you are well intentioned and the teacher isn't just exploiting you for easy sex or ego gratification.

When a student-teacher relationship evolves into a romance, the odds of it not working, and of creating lots of misery and regret, are very high. Think of all the reasons not to sleep with your boss or your therapist; then triple the potential for disaster.

Now let's consider a very different scenario. You and your partner have been married—or in a committed relationship—for years. Your partner is a spiritual teacher, or later becomes one, and you say to them, "I want to be your student as well as your mate." By then, if the relationship is a healthy one, each of you knows the other very well and has few illusions about the other. In this case it may be possible to build a strong student-teacher relationship on top of that foundation—just as it would be atop a good friendship. There are some potentially serious dangers and difficulties, but—if both people are wise and loving—those dangers and difficulties can sometimes be navigated.

Of course, both of you have to agree to such a relationship. You might say to your partner, "I want to be your student," and they might say, "I love you with all my heart, but no." They might even say, "No, my darling—*because* I love you with all my heart."

I feel a very strong attraction to a particular spiritual teacher. It's an emotional and spiritual attraction, not a sexual one. Is this a good reason for me to become their student? Or is it a good reason to be cautious—or to back off entirely? Should I tell the teacher how I feel about them?

Don't deny or repress your attraction, and don't make a big deal out of it. Accept it temporarily as part of your life, like the smells emanating from the coffee shop near your home. Keep observing this attraction carefully—without acting on it. Then, slowly, over time, let yourself be guided by what you experience with the teacher.

Here's what *not* to do. Don't hurl yourself at the teacher's feet. Don't swear loyalty to them. And don't hang around them like a groupie.

Attraction—whether it's spiritual, emotional, or sexual—can come from all sorts of places inside us. Some of these places are healthy; some aren't. You might even feel strongly attracted to a teacher *because* they're a potential source of harm. They might remind you—probably unconsciously—of someone who hurt you, such as an abusive parent or relative. They might represent something you lacked and wished for when you grew up. They might have great self-confidence, which may turn out to be overconfidence or narcissism. Or they might just be clever or charming or funny—but not in a loving, mindful way.

If the teacher also takes a strong interest in *you*, I recommend taking a big, overt step backward. The dynamics I've just described—a strong attraction to a teacher, plus the teacher's strong interest in you—are often hallmarks of danger. This could be a charismatic but exploitive teacher who has targeted you. Remove yourself from the situation (and, if possible, the spiritual community) for a week or two. This should enable you to clear your head and take stock.

It's possible, of course, that the teacher's interest in you is entirely benign—or something you imagined. Stepping away for a time may help you sort this out. If you like, discuss your observations and experience with people you trust—ideally, people from both outside and within your spiritual community. Also pay close attention to how your body feels.

After one or two weeks, if it feels safe—and right—to return, by all means do so. But proceed slowly and carefully. Keep your eyes open and your head clear, and continue to pay close attention to your body.

Lots of bad decisions feel right at first. So do lots of wise decisions. But the wise ones *continue* to feel right over time, while the bad ones look worse and worse.

So if you feel a strong urge to pull up stakes and follow a teacher to Alaska or Morocco or Nepal, wait a substantial amount of time (at least three or four months) before deciding whether to act on that impulse. That teacher, and their spiritual community, will almost certainly still be around a few months from now, and there will likely be other opportunities to connect with them.

As for telling your teacher what you feel, I wouldn't say anything for a few months. Then, if the attraction is still strong, either say something or not—whatever feels wisest to you at that point. If you'll feel safer having someone you trust with you, invite them to accompany you.

But whether you say something or not, the teacher probably already knows what you're feeling, just from observing you.

7

Life Balance

Life is all about balance. Since I have only one leg, I understand that well.

NIYA, FROM SANDY FUSSELL'S NOVEL
SHAOLIN TIGER

Balance is not a passive resting place—it takes work, balancing the giving and the taking, the raking out and the putting in.

ROBIN WALL KIMMERER

Control and surrender have to be kept in balance. . . . We've treasured the controlling part of ourselves and neglected the surrendering part.

BRIAN ENO

Almost every wise saying has an opposite one, no less wise, to balance it.

GEORGE SANTAYANA

While it's important to honor the seemingly spiritual side of your life, it's just as important to honor life's everyday aspects.
Whatever roles we agree to play in life, it's our responsibility to juggle or balance them as best we can.

It's easy to imagine that all things ostensibly spiritual—meditation, prayer, religious services, retreats, talks, classes, volunteering, and so on—should take precedence over the more supposedly mundane aspects of life.

Yet we eventually discover that this is a false dichotomy—and that what we call the everyday or the mundane is actually miraculous.

We also come to see that everything in life presents us with an opportunity to engage fully, be of service, and wake up.

Any form of spiritual study or practice takes time—and will likely require you to make changes in your life and your schedule.
Moreover, some of these changes will need to be negotiated with other people.

As your spiritual study and practice evolve, *you* will change as well. This will not always make the people around you happy, and some of your relationships will probably change as a result. Some relationships will likely drop away, and some new ones will begin.

Healthy human relationships are like spines: solid, supportive, and reliable, but also flexible. This flexibility can manifest in many different ways. Sometimes it involves people doing the same thing together. Sometimes it means doing different things in an aligned or synchronized way. Sometimes it means moving in entirely different directions, with each other's blessing and support. Sometimes it involves a major realignment. And sometimes it requires us to let go.

Some of the people you're close to may not understand what it means to study with a spiritual teacher.
Helping an interested person to better understand spiritual practices, teachings, teachers, and traditions

can be a generous, compassionate act. But trying to *make* someone understand usually fails—and creates discord and anxiety.

Similarly, it's always fine to invite someone to meet your teacher or visit your spiritual community. But pressuring them, or trying to convert or recruit them, is deeply disrespectful.

We can and should offer explanations when people ask us for them. But we're not responsible for fixing their misunderstandings.

When you're explaining and getting nowhere with someone, it's usually best to stop explaining. For one thing, the person may simply have lost interest. (You may want to ask them, "Do you want to hear more?" or "Do you want me to try again, or should we just drop it?") And sometimes it's wisest to not explain at all.

With this caveat: it's always best to avoid the dismissive and uncompassionate phrase, "You wouldn't understand."

Whether you explain or not, here's another option: give the person a copy of this book.

Spiritual Community

8

We have all known the long loneliness and we have learned that the only solution is love and that love comes with community.

DOROTHY DAY

A proper community, we should remember also, is a commonwealth: a place, a resource, an economy. It answers the needs, practical as well as social and spiritual, of its members—among them the need to need one another.

WENDELL BERRY

It is only when we stand up, with all our failings and sufferings, and try to support others rather than withdraw into ourselves, that we can fully live the life of community.

JEAN VANIER

But many of us seek community solely to escape the fear of being alone. Knowing how to be solitary is central to the art of loving. When we can be alone, we can be with others without using them as a means of escape.

BELL HOOKS

You can tell a lot about a spiritual teacher from the community that forms around them.
The emotional and spiritual health of a community tends to reflect the emotional and spiritual health of its teachers.

The students of a wise and caring teacher won't all be wise and caring as well—but the spiritual community as a whole will usually be welcoming, supportive, and down-to-Earth. In contrast, a community that forms around a narcissistic or deluded teacher will feel like a fan club, a pep rally, a platoon, or a cult.

That said, spiritual community has its own unique vibes and sensibility. These may reflect energy and fit rather than health or dysfunction. A community can be sane and compassionate, yet feel just right to some folks and not at all right to others.

Here's an example. Not far from my home, there's a popular meditation center whose guiding teacher seems honorable, authentic, and astute. When I go there, though, I feel constricted, exhausted, and antsy. My wife and one of my friends have had the same experience. The vibes of the place are wrong for us.

But the center, and its teacher and community, continue to thrive, and I know several people who find the place enormously energizing. For them, the vibes of the place resonate beautifully. It's a classic case of fit versus the lack of it.

Each spiritual group has its unique etiquette, norms, expectations, quirks, and problems.
When I began seriously studying Zen at the Minnesota Zen Center in 1978, I assumed that we were practicing real, authentic, official Zen. How could this not be the case? Our teacher, Dainin Katagiri, was a Zen monk from Japan. He had spent years in a Zen monastery and had been formally endorsed by his teacher.

I soon discovered that "real, authentic, official Zen" was my own fantasy. Katagiri had indeed exported some of our forms and practices from Japan. But other practices and forms were his adaptations. Still others he made up. Others were made up by his students. Furthermore, some of the "ancient" practices he imported from Japan were only decades old.

In any case, these practices didn't represent Zen; they represented one particular stream of Soto-style Japanese Zen. I might as well have imagined that cheeseburgers authentically represent the full range of American cuisine.

Over the past four decades, I've visited many different spiritual centers, churches, synagogues, and meditation groups—including more than a dozen Zen centers. I've discovered that they're all different. Of course they are.

And each one has its own problems and challenges. The specifics are unique to each organization, but they always involve some combination of interpersonal, spiritual, financial, and/or property issues.

At age twenty-four, when I first showed up at the Minnesota Zen Center, I expected to find a spiritual community that was free of most human problems. What I found instead was a community of human beings with normal human problems who practiced Zen.

The value of a healthy spiritual community isn't that it's free of problems. It's that its members agree to stay connected, engaged, and respectful, no matter what happens, using their spiritual tradition—and each other—for support.

Indeed, one of the most important functions of community is to help its members work together peaceably *despite* their human limitations and foibles. A spiritual community is often most valuable at precisely those times when difficulties arise, conflicts flare, and people are in pain.

A healthy spiritual community can thus be a boon for its members—and the world. But even the healthiest spiritual community won't be Eden, or anything close to it.

There is nothing wrong with a spiritual community soliciting contributions of money or time— but if you are strongly or repeatedly pressured to contribute, be suspicious.

How a spiritual community handles money will tell you a lot about its health.

Almost every spiritual community faces the same ongoing challenge: balancing its accounts without sucking its members dry or harassing them endlessly for contributions. It's often a narrow path.

An organization that isn't consistently financially responsible will soon cease to exist. One that asks too much of its members will burn them out and push them away. As a result, each spiritual community needs to find its own middle way—its own unique combination of fundraising, careful spending and budgeting, dues collection, the sale of products and services, and the sponsorship of events.

Asking members to pay dues—and charging money for classes, workshops, concerts, and other special events—is understandable, and usually necessary. There are also times—when a spiritual community plans a major construction project, for example—when it's appropriate to ask for major donations of time and/or money. But asking you for more than you can afford is heartless and exploitive—especially if the request is made in a high-pressure way.

In a healthy community, people are respectfully asked to donate money and encouraged to volunteer their time—but the number of requests is reasonable. Also, the answer *no, but I'll donate some of my time*—or even simply *no*—is always accepted gracefully.

In an unhealthy community, members are pushed endlessly to donate time, money, and effort—and, usually, the more they give, the more they are asked to give further. The consistent message is, *The teacher and the community matter. Your life doesn't matter as much. Pony up.* If that's the message you receive, consider getting out fast—with your wallet closed and firmly in your pocket.

Rising in the hierarchy of a spiritual community isn't an indicator of your spiritual development or potential.

It's natural for any service organization—especially one that relies heavily on volunteers—to tap whatever talent it has available.

If you become a member of a spiritual community and you've got a valuable skill, there's a good chance you'll be asked to provide it—probably sooner rather than later. Whether that skill is carpentry, bookkeeping, public speaking, event planning, editing, or strategic planning, you may quickly find yourself in a position of influence.

So there you are, editing your spiritual teacher's talks for publication, or helping guide the organization through a five-year visioning process. Does this mean you've got a great deal of spiritual aptitude or achievement? No. It merely means you have a skill the community needs.

I've watched people in spiritual communities strive for (or lust after) ordination, leadership roles, and other positions of authority. I've watched one person be jealous of another because of their appointed role in the community. I've seen unwise and unloving teachers assign people to organizational roles not because of their skills, but as forms of favor, reward, flattery, or punishment. I've known of teachers who have put attractive students in key positions in order to more easily seduce them. All of these actions fly in the face of what a spiritual community should be.

In a healthy community, members serve each other willingly, giving what they can, without regard for status, position, or recognition.

The more secrets a spiritual community keeps, the less healthy it is.

Like the rest of us, a spiritual teacher is entitled to a personal life and a reasonable amount of privacy. We shouldn't monitor teachers when they're in their own homes, or set limits on what they are allowed to think or feel. (And of course, teachers should respect their students' privacy the same way.) But a teacher's—or student's—personal privacy is very different from transparency in their organization and community.

Any spiritual community—and, indeed, any organization concerned with the public good—ought to be honest, transparent, and clear about its rules and norms; its mission or purpose; its finances; its power structure; and what it expects or requires from its members.

When clarity, honesty, or transparency is lacking, people will rightfully assume that its leaders have something to hide—and a reason to hide it.

And when a community operates by two separate sets of rules—one for show (and for the rank and file), the other for its inner circle—then that community is almost always a dangerous cult.

Now a few observations on a different form of secrecy:

Some religious traditions have closely guarded "secret" teachings and rituals that are reserved for a privileged few. Sometimes these are never shared with anyone outside the tradition; sometimes they are also kept secret from almost everyone *within* the tradition as well, except for certain senior folks. Occasionally someone reveals one of these teachings to the outside world, and it always turns out to be underwhelming.*

The idea behind such secrecy is that if a teaching is given to someone who isn't ready for it, they might misuse, abuse, or misconstrue it. Fair enough. But in these cases, what gets called secrecy is actually discernment and discretion.

Any good spiritual teacher needs to work with each student based on that student's insight, temperament, capacity, experience, and background. There's no point in trying to teach something to a student who isn't ready and able to learn it—or to one who may use what they learn to cause harm. Furthermore, there are things that a teacher might say to a student in private that would be unwise to say in a public talk or workshop. (Still, I wish that spiritual teachers and communities would avoid using the term *secret* in such contexts, since it can easily encourage jealousy or confusion.)

---

*I'm privy to a few of these "secret" teachings and rituals. One involves holding out your arms and letting your hands drop to your knees. Another involves laying the corner of your meditation mat on top of your teacher's mat.

There are other situations, though, where a supposed "teaching" is kept secret because it's exploitive or abusive. One of the most damaging of these is the "secret" teaching that involves the teacher having sex with the student. The sanest and most compassionate thing to do if you're offered any such "teaching" is to blow the whistle on it very publicly.

If you move to a residential spiritual community, you will quickly learn that life there is much like life anywhere else.

Many of us move to spiritual communities to find safety, serenity, and respite from the craziness of human life. What we *actually* find are some new and different flavors of craziness. And, usually, most of the old, familiar ones, too.

And if we move to a spiritual community to escape our problems—or our demons, or ourselves—whatever we tried to leave behind will surely follow us there.

This isn't unique to spiritual communities. Whenever we try to flee anything, it tends to turn up wherever we go to hide from it.

One spiritual teacher I know went to a Buddhist monastery for an extended time to escape the travails of endless yearning, seeking, and grasping. He figured he would have few opportunities to yearn, seek, and grasp while following a full, prescribed daily schedule of meditation, study, and manual labor.

It wasn't long before he found himself profoundly attracted to a woman sitting a few cushions away. Soon he spent most of his meditation time yearning for her and thinking about her. He also spent time yearning for his lost ability to meditate—and for a life that was free of yearning.

I don't mean to suggest that living in a residential spiritual community is pointless or unwise. I've lived in intentional communities and spent time in monasteries, and I can affirm that they have a great deal to offer. But one thing they do not—and cannot—offer is escape from the challenges and struggles of being human.

Opening to Life

9

> Our goal should be to live life in radical amaze-
> ment. . . . Get up in the morning and look at the world
> in a way that takes nothing for granted. Everything is
> phenomenal; everything is incredible; never treat life
> casually. To be spiritual is to be amazed.
>
> ABRAHAM JOSHUA HESCHEL

> The whole purpose of wrestling with life is to be trans-
> formed into the self we are meant to become, to step
> out of the confines of our false securities and allow our
> creating God to go on creating. In us.
>
> JOAN CHITTISTER

> We have a choice. We can spend our whole life suffering
> because we can't relax with how things really are, or

we can relax and embrace the open-endedness of the human situation, which is fresh, unfixed, unbiased.

PEMA CHÖDRÖN

Instead of asking "what do I want from life?," a more powerful question is, "what does life want from me?"

ECKHART TOLLE

Learning from a spiritual teacher is serious business—but playfulness is just as essential to a full and open life.

If we don't take life seriously, it will come back at us hard and force us to.

If we *only* take life seriously, we'll become tight, brittle, and a pain in the ass to others.

Any meaningful spiritual inquiry or practice requires commitment, patience, attention, and a seriousness of purpose. Sooner or later, it will also make you laugh at yourself.

Don't stint on the commitment, patience, attention, or seriousness. Please don't stifle the laughter, either.

As Zen teacher Steve Hagen puts it, "We need to live as if waking up is the most important thing in the world—and, simultaneously, not important at all."

As your heart and mind open, you'll likely experience more joy, more suffering, and more of everything else.
Working with a good spiritual teacher will make you more human, not less.

It will make you more aware of your limitations, your uncertainty, your fear, and your vulnerability. This awareness always hurts at first—and it is always profoundly valuable.

Most of us show up on spiritual teachers' doorsteps because we want our spiritual and emotional pain to go away. Sooner or later, though, we have to make a choice. We can use our relationship with a spiritual teacher as a way to blunt our pain or protect ourselves from it. Or we can use the relationship to help us lean *into* that pain, work through it, and come out the other side.

What's on the other side? No one knows until they get there—and it's different for each person and each situation. But our teachers often know—and can help guide us there.

If you have a seemingly powerful spiritual experience, enjoy it—then let it go.

The more energy an experience involves, the more we're inclined to make of it. Because it feels so strong or profound, we assume it must also be deeply significant. But that's not always so.

In 1974, while doing sun salutations, I experienced the void. My body, my sense of self, and the entire physical world disappeared. There was nothing but universal, timeless vibration.

Then everything reappeared. I stood there in amazement, slack-jawed and speechless, wondering how much time had passed. (Four seconds, it turned out.)

My body will never forget those four seconds. But the experience involved very little insight. It gave me a visceral sense that the universe is nothing but vibration. That was nice. But people learn this (in principle) in high-school physics.

In contrast, it took me decades to understand just how uncertain life is—and how that uncertainty is an unavoidable part of the human condition. That understanding now permeates my body, but it seeped through slowly, subtly, and incrementally for years.

It's important not to confuse voltage with wisdom.

This is a particularly thorny issue for those of us who have spiritual teachers. We can easily fall into a habit of chasing after "peak" or "powerful" or "spiritual" experiences—deep bliss and serenity, energy rushing up our spine, profound love in our heart, tingling throughout our skin, the concentration of energy in our forehead, a palpable experience of Divine presence, and so on. All of these feel great.

But how an experience feels is far less important than what it leaves behind. Does it make us more human? More empathetic? More generous? More open? More connected to other people? To the world? To the Dharma or the Divine?

Another common pitfall is imagining that these experiences can be reliably induced in some way— e.g., through meditation, prayer, chanting, deep breathing, yoga, Sufi dancing, or some other spiritual exercise.

At first it may seem like practice A leads to experience B. But over time it becomes clear that things aren't that linear. Peak experiences often arise spontaneously. When we attempt to create them, they often prove elusive, no matter how hard we try.

A bigger delusion is imagining that our spiritual teacher can—and should—somehow induce such experiences in us. When we believe this, we relinquish our own discernment and power, and we open ourselves to exploitation. We'll be attracted to unethical teachers who promise us all kinds of spiritual goodies if only we do exactly what they tell us to.

All experiences—spiritual and otherwise, powerful and otherwise—are by nature transitory. They arise, they live in and through us for a time, and then they blow away. As they blow away, the wisest thing we can do is simply watch them and let them dissolve—and be open to whatever arises next.

As you work with a spiritual teacher, you may need to adapt or let go of beliefs and assumptions you've held for years.
Faith and belief are often presented as similar—or even identical. In fact, they are opposites.

Faith is a mix of openness, awareness, recognition, and a willingness to grow and be guided. Faith is born of experience and observation. Belief is the clinging to an idea.

Faith is an unfolding process. Beliefs and assumptions are static objects.

Beliefs and assumptions can be useful as temporary placeholders or hypotheses. But as your faith and insight grow, you will likely discover that some of your long-standing beliefs and assumptions hold you back—and need to be changed or jettisoned. (You may also discover that certain other beliefs have been affirmed by your experience—and have grown into faith.)

You probably came to a spiritual teacher hoping to deepen your faith. If your teacher is wise, as part of this process they encouraged you to examine and question many of the things you long took for granted. Eventually, they will help you see *all* beliefs and assumptions as temporary, provisional placeholders, to be dropped when it becomes clear that they don't match reality.

As your faith deepens, something else will likely happen: your doubt will *also* grow or deepen.

This is not a problem to be fixed or avoided. It's a natural part of growth.

I encourage you to welcome in the doubt rather than treat it like a criminal. Examine and question your doubts, just as you would your beliefs and assumptions. Talk honestly with your teacher about them. Follow them and see where they lead. You will discover that doubts may change your faith, but they will never separate you from it.

A Zen proverb puts it this way: *Spiritual practice requires three things: great faith, great doubt, and great determination.*

Almost everyone who has a spiritual teacher goes through a crisis of faith or a dark night of the soul. This may involve the teacher, your relationship with them, or both.
A spiritual crisis is a form of death and rebirth—and an essential, and often painful, part of growing up.

When a spiritual crisis looms, your impulse may be to turn and run in the opposite direction. Don't. Settle yourself, take a deep breath, and step forward into it.

At least one of these crises will likely involve your spiritual teacher.

If you're like most of us, you will discover that the teacher is not who you thought they were. They may reveal a shadow side—or a blind spot, limitation, or character flaw—that you hadn't seen before. This discovery is always valuable, because it involves letting go of a belief or assumption in favor of reality.

Or perhaps someday what you will feel called to do will fly in the face of what your teacher wants or expects of you—or what the two of you had planned. (This is quite common.)

If you're serious about getting to the bottom of things, you'll probably have several such crises in your life. These may shock and surprise you. They will surely hurt like hell. And you'll come out of each one a wiser person.

Sometimes spiritual study and practice can be surprisingly boring.

The same can be said of childhood, marriage, and parenthood.

Life is one unfolding miracle after another. It's also completely ordinary. They're two aspects of one process. Working with a spiritual teacher isn't exempt from this process.

Some folks come to a spiritual teacher looking for excitement, which they often redefine as spiritual growth. For a time, they may even find—or generate—the excitement they seek. But eventually life with the teacher will have its stretches of boredom and apparent stagnation. That's because it's life—not some more exciting alternative to it. This is the point where spiritual thrill seekers typically bail out and flee the teacher.

You've probably met some people who flit from teacher to teacher—or from lover to lover, job to job, city to city, or religion to religion—as soon as the excitement in their life wanes. These folks usually present themselves as wanderers or adventurers. In fact, they're afraid of life—and terrified of simply being with it in moments of calm and monotony.

No matter who your own teacher is, you will have your own periods of monotony and calm. Please hang in throughout these periods, for they will prove essential to your process of growing up.

Stay present as well—because, at any moment, monotony can open into miracles.

Saying Goodbye

10

The path of spiritual apprenticeship eventually leads away from a teacher's physical company to our own tasks of living an enlightened life.

GREG BOGART

The question is not will *we become disillusioned by spiritual practice, it is* when. *Our disappointments can be broad and shallow or pointed and deep. Their circumference will often include the teacher, the spiritual community, and the very practice itself.*

JOHN KAIN

Leave if you must. But leave when you are strong, not weak. Leaving should be a choice and not the only option.

RAM MOHAN

There's a trick to the Graceful Exit. It begins with the vision to recognize when a job, a life stage, a relationship is over—and to let go. It means leaving what's over without denying its value.

ELLEN GOODMAN

There is nothing wrong with changing spiritual teachers.
In fact, in most religions there is a long and respected tradition of doing so.

A student-teacher relationship is not a marriage or a mortgage. You're under no obligation to continue it if it no longer serves you—or no longer helps you serve the world.

Indeed, people leave their spiritual teachers and find new ones all the time, and they have done so for millennia.

Buddhism was founded by a fellow who walked away from his spiritual teachers and began anew. Roughly 1,700 years later, the Japanese Buddhist monk Dogen sailed to China from Japan, convinced that there were no authentic Buddhist teachers in his country. He eventually found the real thing in the Chinese teacher Rujing.

One of my own former teachers often said, "The final task of the teacher is to free the student of the teacher."

Actually, I'd rephrase this a bit. Yes, freeing the student from the teacher is the final phase of a healthy student-teacher relationship. But the teacher can't free the student; the student needs to free themselves. The teacher can, however, support that separation and offer their blessing.

When you sense clearly that it's time to move on, set your affairs in order, say a respectful goodbye, and go.

But with one caveat: don't fool yourself. Lots of people pick up and go when circumstances—or their teachers—finally force them to face aspects of themselves that they don't want to examine, and may have avoided for a long time. This is precisely when they need to *not* run away, but stay right where they are, step into what they've been avoiding (including the accompanying pain), and let things unfold.

When you feel an urge to leave your teacher, use your powers of discernment with yourself. Do you want to leave because you're hurt or afraid and want to feel better? Do you sense imminent pain or fear on the horizon and hope to get out of its way? In either case, take a deep breath and stay put. (Unless, of course, the source of your pain or fear is an exploitive teacher. In that case, take your leave ASAP.)

It may also be wise to get the advice of people you trust, both inside and outside your spiritual community, before making a break.

By the way, it's not just common to change spiritual teachers; throughout history, it's also been common for people to move from one spiritual tradition to another. The list of folks who broke away from the fold includes Abraham, Buddha, Jesus, Paul, Muhammad, and countless others. If you make such a choice yourself, consider yourself in good company.

I should add that ending your student-teacher relationship with someone doesn't necessarily mean ending *any* relationship with them. Over time, the two of you might become trusted colleagues, or friends, or confidants.

A teacher who is right for you today may no longer be right for you a month, a year, or a decade from now.

There may come a time when there is nothing more that your teacher can help you with—perhaps because of your own limitations, perhaps because of theirs.

Or you and your teacher may begin leaning in incompatible directions. Or you may outgrow your teacher. Or the two of you may simply grow apart, as sometimes happens with friends.

The change that ends your relationship with your teacher may not even have anything to do with you. I know a deeply committed spiritual teacher who realized, after some years, that her calling had changed. Once she felt sure of this, she announced to her students, "I'll be stepping down from my teaching role shortly. I feel called to focus my efforts on reducing human trafficking instead." Soon afterward, she was gone from the community.

When any of these occurs, don't fight it or try to fix it. Accept it and respectfully say goodbye.

If you reach a place where you get stuck, you may need to find a different teacher to get unstuck.

Getting stuck is underrated. Sometimes being stuck is exactly what we most need. Behind the stuckness, energy can build for a breakthrough or transformation. Not always, but often.

Being stuck indefinitely, though, usually means that a change is necessary. Sometimes it means changing teachers.

There's no formula for navigating this. But if you relate to the world today very much the way you did two years ago, and your relationship with your teacher has remained the same as well, there's a good chance you're due for a shake-up.

Finding a new teacher doesn't necessarily mean leaving your current one. You might stay right where you are but also sign up for retreats or workshops with other teachers. Or, rather than break with your teacher, you might take a couple of months off to visit other teachers and only then decide what to do.

If you do end your relationship with your current teacher, there's no rule that prevents you from returning. (Unless the teacher banishes, punishes, or shames you—in which case ending the relationship was *exactly* the wise thing to do.)

Throughout all this, watch you own mind and use your discernment. Make sure that getting unstuck is not your excuse to flee or avoid something you don't want to face.

It's rarely wise to impulsively leave your spiritual teacher and take up with a different one.
It's rarely wise to suddenly and impulsively do almost anything.

It's possible that you'll meet a spiritual teacher—or read one of their books or watch one of their videos—and immediately think, *This is the one!*

This can happen with a romantic partner, or with a home when you're house hunting, so of course it can happen with a spiritual teacher as well.

But there's a world of difference between *This is the one! Let me take a closer look* and *This is the one! I need to leap forward with my eyes closed!* The first is an internal call to investigate further and use your powers of discernment. The second is an impulse to avoid using those powers.

We all know what happens to folks who make sudden, impulsive decisions about lovers and homes. Many eventually learn that *This is it!* actually means *This is a form of future misery that feels comfortingly familiar.* Others discover that the person or home *is* right for them—but that they would have been wiser to proceed more slowly and carefully. (A small handful of folks simply get lucky—but that's in spite of their impulsiveness, not because of it.)

If you feel a strong, sudden connection to a spiritual teacher, note it. Then proceed carefully, one step at a time. The stronger the pull, the slower and more careful you should be. Remember that this feeling of connection can be a recognition of something deeply valuable—or something deeply toxic. Or even both at once.

A sudden leap away from your old teacher is as ill-advised as a sudden leap toward a new one. If your current teacher is abusive or exploitative, of course get away ASAP. Otherwise, though, it's rude—and not in your own best interests—to simply disappear on them.

Instead, if you do decide to end the relationship, it's usually best to withdraw slowly and incrementally, over a period of weeks or months. This gives you time to weigh your options and make decisions; to gradually end or reassess relationships with community members; to respectfully explain to the teacher that you are moving on, and thank them for their guidance; to complete any short-term volunteer commitments you may have made; and to give the community time to find someone to take your place.

If and when it is time to leave your teacher, you will know it.

This realization may come as a sudden insight, or it may slowly work its way into you. Either way, don't fight it, deny it, argue with it, or try to brush it away. Just observe it and let it be for a time.

If it's a momentary impulse, it will soon drift away. But if it's an important insight, it will stick with you—or keep returning.

Once you do know that it's time to leave, it's best to neither hurry nor dawdle. Make your preparations carefully and respectfully. Complete what needs to be completed. Then say goodbye and go.

This departure will probably be stressful—and perhaps even emotionally wrenching. For many people, it can be like losing a close friend or relative. Let yourself grieve the loss. It may also be wise for you to talk with a good friend or counselor about the transition.

If you plan to move out of the immediate area, it may still be possible to continue studying with your current teacher. The same may be true if *they* move away.

Yes, there is something uniquely valuable about face-to-face contact. But there is nothing truly essential about it.

Ask your teacher if they're willing to continue to work with you at a distance. Offer as many options for this as possible: Skype, phone, email, etc. In the twenty-first century, many spiritual teachers will say yes—though you never know which forms of connection they'll prefer to use.

If you do create a long-distance student-teacher relationship, try to find a way to meet with them in person occasionally as well. Different teachers will have different views on frequency, but I suggest meeting face-to-face at least once or twice a year, if possible.

If your teacher gets angry or offended because you are planning to leave—or if they exert undue pressure on you to remain—you may need to end the relationship quickly.
Let's revisit Steve Hagen's observation from the beginning of chapter 4:

> A good teacher won't need you. They won't need (or expect) you to stay with them, and they won't be personally invested in what you do or the choices you make.

A spiritual teacher's job, after all, is to serve you and help you serve the world. If they're upset about your upcoming departure, it means they're more focused on what you can do for them or their community.

If this is the case, there may soon be some fallout—accusations, recriminations, shaming, or even shunning. Keep your eyes open—and be prepared to leave sooner than you had planned.

If possible, leave the door open to return, even if right now returning seems unimaginable.
Life can take unpredictable turns. Broken relationships sometimes heal. Estranged relatives reconcile. Divorced couples reunite and remarry. Occasionally, students and their teachers separate and later get back together.

There are some times in life when a bridge needs to be burned because something deeply dangerous is hurtling across it toward you. If this genuinely describes your situation, grab a torch and set the bridge ablaze.

Otherwise, though, it's wiser to simply say goodbye and walk away, leaving the bridge intact.

With or without a spiritual teacher, your life is always precious and full of possibility.

The end of any important relationship engenders strong (and sometimes contradictory) emotions: grief, sorrow, loneliness, regret, relief, release, and, sometimes, even joy. Let yourself feel all of these as they bubble up. Then let them go. When they arise anew, let them in and let them go again. And again.

You may or may not have another spiritual teacher in your life some day. Don't assume that there won't—or will—be another.

Whatever has happened, and whatever else you feel, also don't assume you've reached a dead end. Endings often turn into—or point the way to—new beginnings.

What's next? You don't know. No one knows. No one ever knows. We *can't* know, because we are created beings who live inside of time. We can only live into the next moment, and the next, and the next, with all the wisdom and compassion we can muster.

With or without a teacher, this is always our situation, our responsibility, and our privilege.

Journey wisely. Journey well.

APPENDIX

When You're the New Kid at the Spiritual Center

Imagine this:

You stand in the doorway of a strange building, surrounded by unfamiliar sights, sounds, and smells. You wonder what to do, what to say, what questions to ask, and how to get to know the people inside. Perhaps those people dress strangely or use unfamiliar (or even unrecognizable) words and phrases.

This scenario gets acted out daily at spiritual, religious, and meditation centers around the world.

Here is some brief, down-to-Earth guidance for anyone contemplating such an encounter. It covers what questions to ask, what etiquette to follow, what to look for, what to avoid, what to keep in mind, and when to turn around and leave.

➤ **Call or email before you visit.** The center's hours may be unusual or irregular, or it may be staffed only at certain times. Many centers offer regular orientations or introductory sessions; ask if one of these will be held soon.

➤ **Don't be afraid or intimidated.** A visit to a meditation or spiritual center may be surprising, disappointing, exhilarating, enlightening, or disillusioning—but it will almost never be immediately dangerous.

➤ When you first visit a center or group, everyone but you will know how to act, what to say, and what is going on in general. The best thing you can do is be straightforward. **Say, "I'm new here and need some guidance."** Most folks in a healthy community will be happy to help you.

➤ **Be honest and straightforward.** Speak and act as you normally do, unless you are asked to do otherwise.

➤ **Dress in loose, comfortable, somewhat modest clothing.** This will help make any spiritual practice (meditation, stretching, kneeling, etc.) as easy and comfortable as possible. Dressing on the modest and conservative side will also help you adhere to any dress code. (At some centers, no one will care what you wear; at others, people may care quite a bit.) Once you arrive, you may be asked to remove your shoes. You might also be given a head covering, a prayer shawl, a robe, or some other ritual garment to put on.

➤ **Observe the organization's etiquette.** You may be asked to observe silence for a short period, or perform a few formal bows. Follow others' lead unless doing so will be painful, or harmful to yourself or others. Feel free to ask later about the purpose or proper form of any practice or ritual.

➤ **If you are asked to do something you have genuine ethical or religious objections to, don't do it;** simply stand or sit quietly until the ritual is complete. And if you're asked to do something clearly inappropriate, such as profess your love and loyalty to the resident teacher, politely refuse and quickly leave.

➤ At the appropriate time (usually at the end of your visit), **ask any questions you like.** Feel free to ask both practical questions ("What are these cushions for?") and spiritual ones ("How does this practice relate to the Golden Rule?"). If you don't understand an answer, ask for clarification.

➤ **Request more information if you like.** Ask for a tour of the center, for a copy of its schedule of activities, a web address, and/or any free brochures or pamphlets. These may not be offered automatically.

➤ **If you'd like beginning instruction in the group's spiritual practices, don't be shy about asking for it.** You may be offered this instruction on the spot. More likely, though, you'll be asked to come back at another time, typically for an introductory workshop or session. This will normally be brief (an hour or two) and either free or inexpensive. There may also be a longer class, workshop, or retreat for new folks who want a more in-depth introduction.

➤ **Be wary of requests for money.** Spiritual centers have bills to pay like everyone else, so you may be asked for a donation or a pledge. But it's fine to say "not today" or "let me think on it and decide later."

➤ **Always feel free to leave.** No one can keep you there if you don't want to stay—and it's unlikely that anyone will try. When you want or need to go, simply say goodbye and leave—or just leave discreetly and silently. No justifications or explanations are needed.

If you like what you experience, come back to test the waters some more. If you don't, try visiting someplace else.

No two spiritual groups or centers are alike, even when they're in the same tradition. As with so many other things in life, it's wise to test the waters slowly and carefully, to explore and compare multiple options, and to practice discernment at all times.

Useful Resources

On the Web

➤ spiritualteachers.org

A quirky, helpful site run by Shawn Nevins that features articles, links, and an excellent essay, "Guidelines for Choosing a Spiritual Teacher." The site includes Nevins' ratings and highly personal reviews of more than fifty past and present spiritual teachers. While these are interesting and often insightful, take them with plenty of salt.

➤ holyrascals.com

An even quirkier site run by Rami Shapiro (and others) that offers videos, interviews with spiritual teachers and writers, and an eclectic mix of items by and about spiritual teachers from many different traditions. The videos alone include Joan Borysenko, Matthew Fox, Andrew Harvey, Seyedih Nahid Angha, Monty Python's John Cleese, and others.

➤ guruphiliac.blogspot.com

A site devoted to the outing of false and corrupt spiritual teachers, especially gurus. Its credo is *Revealing self-aggrandizement and superstition in self-realization since 2005*. It is snarky, sometimes funny, and often eye-opening.

Books

➤ *A Rare and Precious Thing: The Possibilities and Pitfalls of Working with a Spiritual Teacher* by John Kain

A brilliant, wide-ranging, and deeply insightful book—as well as a surprisingly easy and lively read. Kain profiles eight spiritual teachers who represent a wide range of traditions. He also offers pithy, penetrating essays on subjects such as boundaries, disillusionment, and leaving the teacher, as well as a fine collection of pertinent quotations. If you've found *The User's Guide to Spiritual Teachers* useful, read Kain's book next. (One important caveat: several of the spiritual teachers whom Kain profiles or quotes—and obviously deeply respects—have been the subjects of scandals. Kain's book thus serves as a reminder that we all need to practice ongoing discernment.)

➤ *In the Company of Sages: The Journey of the Spiritual Seeker* by Greg Bogart. An earlier edition was published under the title *The Nine States of Spiritual Apprenticeship.*

A helpful and detailed guide to the student-teacher relationship, as well as a deeply perceptive roadmap of what Bogart calls the nine stages of spiritual apprenticeship. Bogart highlights many different traditions, and covers a great deal of ground, in highly readable prose. He is consistently open-hearted and fair-minded—sometimes too fair-minded. Like Kain, he quotes and honors many spiritual teachers who lived very morally questionable lives. This is particularly evident in his chapters "Testing" and "Grace and Guru Yoga," in which Bogart sometimes allows narcissism and sociopathy to pass for "crazy wisdom" or "wild and inscrutable behavior." Please read these two chapters with healthy skepticism. As Bogart himself writes in a later chapter, "We're also wise to consider the possibility that some so-called crazy-wisdom teaching is in fact inappropriate conduct. Teachers may fall into traps they hadn't foreseen, even if their strange actions are attributed to crazy wisdom."

➤ *Sex and the Spiritual Teacher* by Scott Edelstein

A down-to-Earth investigation of spiritual teachers who have sex with their students: how and why it happens, why it's so common, and the suffering that such encounters often cause. Part 1 looks at why spiritual teachers are sexy, the spiritual teacher as alpha figure and role model, sex as a spiritual teaching, tantra and pseudo-tantra, the shadow side of celibacy, and many other interrelated issues. Part 2 discusses what can be done—by students, teachers, spiritual communities, and other organizations—to limit spiritual teachers' misconduct.

➤ *Eyes Wide Open: Cultivating Discernment on the Spiritual Path* by Mariana Caplan
➤ *Halfway Up the Mountain: The Error of Premature Claims to Enlightenment* by Mariana Caplan

Read these brilliant, honest books in sequence, with *Eyes Wide Open* first.

Eyes Wide Open is a deeply wise and beautifully written investigation of discernment. Caplan addresses nearly every relevant issue in a penetrating and forthright way. Her topics include student-teacher relationships, self-deception, projection, spiritual materialism (using "spiritual" techniques to strengthen egocentricity and/or an attachment to spiritual "accomplishment"), spiritual bypassing (using "spirituality" to sidestep personal, emotional unfinished business), spiritually transmitted diseases (common obstacles that get in the way), and many others. *Eyes Wide Open* brims with understanding and compassion.

Halfway Up the Mountain is also about discernment on the spiritual path. However, it focuses on one of the path's most common, tempting, and potentially dangerous pitfalls: believing ourselves to be wiser than we actually are. Caplan alternates between her own highly perceptive analysis and the astute observations of dozens of spiritual teachers.

I do *not* recommend Caplan's *The Guru Question: The Perils and Rewards of Choosing a Spiritual Teacher* (previously published in 2002 under the title *Do You Need a Guru?*), which is by turns wise, delusional, and painfully melodramatic. Particularly off the mark is Caplan's epilogue, "An Unexpected Twist: False Complaints About Teachers."

How is it possible for the same human being to write two of the most valuable and profound books about the spiritual path, as well as one that goes so far off the rails? Caplan herself has the answer: "[A]bsolutely no one, including teachers and ourselves, is exempt from the pitfalls one inevitably encounters on the spiritual path" (*Eyes Wide Open*, p. 9).

Some Final Words of Gratitude

My agent, Barbara Moulton, had the wisdom to connect me with the folks at Wisdom Publications, which turned out to be the ideal publisher for this book.

My editor at Wisdom, Josh Bartok (who is both a spiritual teacher and an editor), helped to make this the best and most useful book possible. He's the sharpest, wisest editor I've ever had.

My wife, Ariella Tilsen, pushed me repeatedly to finish the book in the face of a hundred important (and four hundred unimportant) distractions.

My heartfelt thanks to them all.

"When You're the New Kid at the Spiritual Center" first appeared, in slightly different form, in the magazine *The Edge*, and on its website, edgemagazine .net, under the title "10 Tips for the New Kid at the Spiritual Center." The article also appeared in the March 7, 2011, issue of the *New Age Journal* online at newagejournal.com. The article is copyright © 2011 by The Edge Magazine.

About the Author

Since 1978, Scott Edelstein has studied happily and productively with several spiritual teachers. As the friend of many spiritual teachers from a variety of traditions, he has also spent much time with them "off duty," sometimes acting as confidant.

Scott has served as editor and literary agent for several spiritual teachers, including Steve Hagen (author of *Buddhism Plain and Simple, Meditation Now or Never*, and other books) and Rami Shapiro (author of *The Sacred Art of Lovingkindness, Minyan, Recovery: The Sacred Art*, and other books).

In 2011, Wisdom Publications published Scott's highly acclaimed *Sex and the Spiritual Teacher: Why It Happens, When It's a Problem, and What We All Can Do.* Natalie Goldberg, author of *Writing Down the Bones*, said of this book, "Anyone who has a spiritual teacher, or hopes to have one someday, should read this book." Jean Illsley Clarke, author of *Self-Esteem: A Family Affair*, wrote, "This is the book we should all read before we need it."

Scott has also published fifteen other books on a wide range of subjects. His work on spiritual topics has appeared in *Shambhala Sun*, *American Jewish World*, *The Writer*, the anthology *What About God?* (Upper Room Books), and elsewhere.

He is a longtime practitioner of both Buddhism and Judaism, and a committed proponent of serious spirituality in all forms and traditions. He has been a member of Methodist, Quaker, Buddhist, and Jewish congregations.

For more about Scott and his books, go to scott edelstein.com.

What to Read Next
from Wisdom Publications

Sex and the Spiritual Teacher
Why It Happens, When It's a Problem, and What We All Can Do
Scott Edelstein

"Well worth reading."—Steve Hagen, author of *Buddhism Plain & Simple*

Living Mindfully
At Home, at Work, and in the World
Deborah Schoeberlein David

"Simple, direct, and full of real-world wisdom, Deborah's excellent new book is for everyone interested in bringing mindful awareness into their daily lives."—Susan Kaiser Greenland, author of *The Mindful Child*

The Grace in Living
Recognize It, Trust It, Abide in It
Kathleen Dowling Singh

"Many of us journey through life unaware of the grace, the freely given blessings, that surround us at every moment—the height of cosmic ingratitude. In *The Grace in Living*, Kathleen Dowling Singh shows us how to break this spell of unawareness. This is an instruction manual on opening our heart to a life that is richer, more meaningful, and joyful. It is difficult to imagine that anyone would not benefit from this luminous book." —Larry Dossey, MD, author of *One Mind*

What's Wrong with Mindfulness (And What Isn't)
Zen Perspectives
Barry Magid
Robert Rosenbaum

"This book is the best thing I've read on mindfulness and the mindfulness movement."—David Loy, author of *A New Buddhist Path*